IN CHRIST'S STEAD

Arthur John Gossip
M.A. (Edin.)

REGENT COLLEGE PUBLISHING
Vancouver, British Columbia

In Christ's Stead by Arthur James Gossip
Copyright © 1925 by Arthur John Gossip
Reproduced by permission of Hodder and Stoughton

Reprinted 2016 with a new introduction
by Regent College Publishing
5800 University Boulevard
Vancouver, BC V6T 2E4 Canada
www.regentpublishing.com

Regent College Publishing is an imprint of the Regent
Bookstore <www.regentbookstore.com>. Views expressed in
works published by Regent College Publishing are those of the
author and do not necessarily represent the official position of
Regent College <www.regent-college.edu>.

These lectures were delivered to the students of the colleges of
the United Free Church of Scotland in Edinburgh, Glasgow,
and Aberdeen

ISBN 978-1-57383-389-9

Cataloguing in Publication information is available from Library and Archives Canada.

FOREWORD

A rthur John Gossip was born in Glasgow in 1879 and was educated at the University of Edinburgh. He spent most of his ministry in his native land of Scotland. He pastored churches in Glasgow and Aberdeen and Fairfax. In 1928 he became professor of Practical Theology and Christian Ethics in Trinity College Glasgow. During the time he was there Trinity became a part of Glasgow University and he was given a chair at that university. He retired from teaching in 1945 and died in 1954.

Scotland has given us many famous preachers, most recently James Stewart. Arthur John Gossip preceded him by a generation and was one of the greatest. This book is a condensation of the Warwick Lectures, which he delivered to the students from the United Free Church of Scotland in the Universities of Glasgow, Edinburgh, and Aberdeen. They were published in 1925 for the first time, again in 1960, and now we are blessed in having them published again this year.

Arthur Gossip had a passion for preaching and that is reflected in this book. This book is composed of six chapters in which he discusses the role of the preacher, the basis of preaching and the object of the sermon, and other aspects of preaching.

Needless to say, the genius of Gossip cannot be reduced to one characteristic. He wrote his sermons word for word, so he always had a manuscript, but he took only an outline into the pulpit. His use of images rivals the Old Testament prophets Isaiah and Jeremiah. He is a wizard with words. For example, on the very first page is this vivid description of his visit to the war front: "I was going to see the war. First I perched high on a motor lorry hurling through the battlefield. I met a friendly sergeant, a loquacious bibulous and without a smattering of culture and with a poverty of language unbelievable—using two ungainly overdriven adjectives of vivid hue that were never rested even for one moment."

His sermons were both thematic and exegetical. On his first pass through preaching through the books of the Bible he laid a foundation for his two-volume commentary on Jeremiah, a one-volume commentary on Isaiah, and a two-volume commentary on the Twelve Minor Prophets.

He urges preachers to make their messages their own message from their own life, faith, and experiences so that his listeners could identify with him.

His preaching style was another secret of his greatness. One listener said, "He often spoke in breathless sentences in which clause was piled on clause and the bounds of syntax were strained in a way no grammarian would have allowed. And yet each clause added its own quota to fan the forces of eloquence until every heart in the eon-gregation was wanned to a generous glow." One needs to read his sermons alongside this book. And the book will no longer be a mere textbook. Reading Arthur Gossip will make one want to become a preacher.

He did not attempt to deal with the philosophies or the theology of sin and evil in the world. He spoke to people to help them move through a world of suffering and evil.

His belief that teaching was to speak to the emotions and hurts of people are well illustrated in the conclusion of his most famous sermon, "When Life Tumbles In." He said, "I do not understand this life of ours but still less can I comprehend how people in trouble and loss and be-reavement can fling away peevishly from the Christian faith. In God's name fleeing to what? Have we not lost enough without losing that too?"

† Dr. Calvin L. Phillips
Past President, Emmanuel School of Religion
Johnson City, Tennessee

Introduction

Arthur John Gossip (1873-1954)
In Christ's Stead

Gossip served pastorates in Liverpool, England; Forfar, Glasgow, and Aberdeen, Scotland; and then was appointed Professor of Christian Ethics and Practical Theology at Trinity Theological College, Glasgow. There in the last stadium of his life he taught and inspired students with a zeal for the proclamation of the gospel.

Selections of his sermons are found in The Scholar as Preacher series and include "The Galilean Accent," "From the Edge of the Crowd," "The Hero in thy Soul," as well as a choice book on prayer, *In the Secret Place of the Most High.*

Delivery of the sermon was extempore. With a card holding an outline and few notes the preacher began quietly and slowly until he caught fire and he was off in a rapid speed with words cascading in torrents. Quotations and illustrations came out of a fertile mind stored from wide reading. Thereafter, Gossip would write out the sermon, preferring to see it on paper after delivering it.

This book is the substance of the Warrack Lectures and both in title and felicity of expression the spirit of Gossip is discerned. He is a man convinced that preaching is only possible as an ambassador for Christ, standing among men, pleading Christ's cause. The pithy and ardent words come from a spiritual sensitivity to human need and deep insight into divine resources. His sermon given after the death of his wife, "When Life Tumbles In, What Then?" lives on — for preaching to him was preaching to your own heart and therefore a shared experience.

RALPH G. TURNBULL

Contents

" Believe me, it takes no little effrontery to engage to reach a helping hand to the struggling, to provide counsel for the uncertain, and light for the blind, and hope for the discouraged, and new heart for the tired. These are, indeed, proud achievements, if the thing works out. But the project grows ridiculous if it all comes to nothing. Yet, in truth, I am not out to prescribe rules for others, rather to lay bare the working of my own mind. Let the man to whom it seems good adopt it. But whoever does not like it, why, let him toss it aside. Though, I confess, I am fain to be helpful to as many of my fellows as I can."—PETRARCH.

" It is the duty of a good man at least to strive to teach others those sound lessons which the spite of time or fortune hath hindered him from executing, so that, many have learned them, some better loved by heaven may one day have power to apply them."—MACHIAVELLI.

" It is easier to be wise for others than to be it for oneself."—
ROCHEFOUCAULD.

" I have long discovered that geologists never read each other's works, and that the only object in writing a book is a proof of earnestness."—DARWIN.

VERY vividly do I remember, over the widening gap of years, the interminable journey in a troop train to join my battalion at the front, on Messines ridge, as it happened : and how some brass hats, who chanced to be in the carriage for a while, learning that I was going up for the first time, good-naturedly gave me some kindly advice, all of it true and wholly admirable ; but, as I even then suspected, really outside of my world. For I was going to see the war, not from the exalted position of a staff officer, but from a very different angle, out of my utter insignificance among the rough-and-tumble in the trenches. And, in point of fact, in twenty minutes, perched high on a load of stuff on a motor lorry hurtling that night out of Bailleul, I learned more that I could really use from a friendly sergeant, a loquacious bibulous soul, without a smattering of culture, and with a poverty of language nearly

unbelievable—all his mental processes were
carried through, like ploughing, by two
ungainly, overdriven adjectives of very
vivid hue that moved endlessly up and
down the furrows, and were never rested even
for one moment. Yet the man knew the life
to which I was going through and through,
from long years of intimate experience of it :
and, as he babbled on, things of practical
value to a raw recruit kept oozing out of him
unconsciously. When the committee in charge
of this lectureship offered it to me, within an
hour I had written a prompt refusal, on the
ground that I possess none of the qualifications
required for the task. But, before I could
post it, somehow that sergeant, whose very
existence I had clean forgotten, rose up in
memory with a queer distinctness. And
once more, shy and far from home, feeling
again the sharpness of a box's edge pressed
hard into my back, I was listening in the
darkness to his uncouth voice still droning
on. And that caused me to think again.
For here, too, is it our staff officers, our
brilliant men who move by right in the high

places of the field, and toward whom we all look with an honourable envy, who are likeliest to be helpful to the average man, whose life will not be theirs at all ? Or, at least, ought this lectureship to be reserved exclusively for them ? Might not, now and then, the unwonted apparition of a Jock straight from the trenches, muddied, dishevelled and unkempt, have something not altogether idle to say to new troops moving in for the first time ? For, gentlemen, brace yourself to face it, the horrid truth is this, that, in nine cases out of ten, your glorious dreams are going to end, not in another Black or Sclater, but in a drab affair like me, stolidly putting through the ordinary hack work of the church, and proud to do it ! In view of which fact, might not an unbroken procession of ten-talent lecturers prove somewhat disheartening to the mass of us with only one, which we have to keep burnishing with some diligence, lest it get mislaid. At all events, on his day there was no more electric speaker than Dr. Reith of Glasgow. Several times have I seen him repeat the miracle of the valley of dry bones on a sultry afternoon in the Assembly, when a whole hallful of men, their minds so soaked in talk they could absorb no more, drowsed, dead to the world.   Yet, almost in an instant, at the first sound of his rushing words, they sat alert, eager, tumultuous.   But never was he more eloquent or moving than in an address he gave us at New College on a minister's week. Yet the result was disappointing.   For, urged thereto by a depression that happily wore off, three several men told me that afternoon that they felt they must pull out of the adventure altogether, as evidently the mental equipment required for the ministry was entirely beyond them, and the pace much too hot for them to last it. That is not what we want here.

No doubt, if these men of genius could really let slip to us the secret of their witchery with words, and their power over their fellows, we would insist on having no one else.   But I suspect that, with all their skill, that is beyond them. Had you asked Shakespeare how he wrote Macbeth, whereas to you sitting in his chair, holding his very pen, nothing at all like that occurs, I suppose that he could only have said, " When I thought about the story of Macbeth that is what rose up in my mind, isn't it so with you ? " To which we could only answer, crossly and with emphasis, " No, it is not." So, to take your first lecturer as an illustration, when all is said and done, the one way in which you or I could ever preach like John Hutton is that we, too, should start by being John Huttons, a possibility that nature has ruled out. And we must not sulk over such facts. For surely we are going to lay it down as our first axiom, never to be forgotten, that we are not to be mere shadows, and pale reflections of anyone else, however distinguished, but mean to come to God on our own feet, and think Him out as best we can in our poor human fashion with our own minds, to express in the way natural to us what we ourselves have found from our own first-hand reading and experience. Anything else is certain to be largely futile. For friendship and preaching are alike in this that, to make anything of them, you must be your real self, and even in a way do violence to your natural reserve. Not that you are to be vulgar enough to babble in the pulpit about your own affairs. " Sir, I am sometimes troubled with a disposition to stinginess," Boswell once confessed to Johnson, and received as answer, " So am I, sir, but I do not tell it." Still less are you meant to blab to a whole congregation the holy intimacies of God's kindness to your soul. There is such a thing as seemly reticence. But you must be open, absolutely frank, content to let the others see right into your mind and heart. And if, fearful that there is terribly little there to see, you keep the doors timidly closed, you may become in time quite a skilled house-painter in this kind of thing, but the real art of it is not for you. For it is not the flat mass of thought common to us all, it is the something extra, the touch of you, that is likely to grip the minds to which you happen to appeal, and make things vivid for them.

As Anatole France has it in a striking page, men do not need to be great to arrest the world : " if they have loved something, or believed something, or hoped for something, and if they have left a part of themselves at the end of their pens," that does it. Resolutely you must make up your mind to be yourself, and hold to it. That will involve you in much labour and sore heartache, but, in the end, it will bring you into your own natural kingdom and inheritance.

No doubt there is such a thing as over self-confidence in the pulpit ; and a shocking sight it is. But that is the mean sin of petty souls. Deeper natures are more apt to rob us of their best through a reverence that sinks into slavish imitation, or through a diffidence that does not trust its own mind, that dares not speak out all that it feels in its own way, assuming that, because it is its own, there is no doubt nothing in it, that pulls itself up, falls nervously into step, shamefacedly hides away that unique something it is here to give. We must, of course, study the masters earnestly, seeking to learn from them, both what to do and to avoid. And in that connection may I interpolate

B

that what Matthew Arnold says of poetry is as true of preaching, that you can't really teach it in the abstract, that the best you can do is to bring one face to face with concrete instances of the thing in being, and say " there it is." And if the scholar does not feel its presence for himself, there can be little more to say. We must, I hold, study the masters, but always remembering, in Emerson's phrase, that we must " take ourselves as our portion," and so go our way, not envying those whose gifts lead to far greater popularity, or to more obvious usefulness ; not jostled by an agitated feeling that their way of it evidently is the thing to do into a cramped conformity to what, for us, is unnatural. " Nothing," says Newman, " that is anonymous will preach." No. It must be the definite message of a definite preacher into which he has thrown a definite personality.

I was brought up under Whyte of St. George's, and was honoured all my youth by being allowed an intimate discipleship. But, often as I tried to coax him to it, that delightful talker on all kinds of themes would never speak about methods of preaching. So much so that years of eager gleaning resulted only in this meagre harvest. Ah! you say, cocking your ears at last, this at least is worth hearing, the whole art of preaching by Alexander Whyte! Listen then. First, "Take long holidays." Second, "After service go straight home, and speak to nobody upon the way." Yes, that's all! As a complete guide to the art of which he was so subtle a master that is perhaps inadequate, with some obvious lacunæ. I suspect, indeed, that you might follow it with scrupulous exactness, might take much longer holidays than he did, and move home resolutely silent, and acquire thereby the reputation, not of a great preacher, but merely of a lazy loafer and of a grumpy boor!

The fact is, of course, that his real teaching on the subject was his stubborn refusal to teach at all, his obvious fear of even seeming to lay his rules on any other, his dread of smothering the younger man's personality, his insistence that in every preacher there should be something quite unique and first-hand and original, and that it is that something that is likely to be of value.

When I was in my first charge in Liverpool, Dods sent me a copy, on its publication, of Caird's University Sermons. Whereat my mind, stunned by the splendour of the thinking and the glory of the language, grew sick with remorseful sorrow for my own folk condemned to listen, kindly souls, to my poor stammering, when, conceivably, they might have been hearing that ! But Dods had little patience with my whimpers of self-pity, sent me a curt postcard—" There are those whom God can reach through John Caird : there are others He can reach through you. You may safely assume that the Divine Mind knows its business, and sends the right man to the right sphere. Get on with your own job in your own way."

What Raleigh said of poets is as true of preachers, " That a poet should be made from other poets without opening his eyes on life and the world is inconceivable." And again, " There is no short cut to the end desired.

Standards, eternal principles, formulæ, sum-
maries, and shibboleths, if they be substituted
for the living experience, are obstacles and
pitfalls. The poet, so far as he is a poet,
accepts nothing on authority. The truths
that he discovers have been discovered by
many before him. What makes them worth
communicating is that he has discovered them
again, reaching them, it may be, by a new
track, but in any case by his own effort, so
that they come to him as the crown of his own
labours, and the fruit of his own sorrows and
struggles and joys."

And so I do not ask you to believe what I
shall say, nor to fall in with my suggestions.
But here are we, gathered together for a little
while. And if, with the usual courtesy, you
young troops moving into the line will listen
to an old campaigner who has knocked about
for five and twenty years, perhaps through
the uncouthness something not unhelpful
may find its way to you. And if that is not
so, if you are merely bored, if, as well may
happen, like Barrie's students after the first
lecture in the mathematical class you fade

out, murmuring, "Let us away, this is no place for us," blame me, and not the committee. For, audacious creatures though they are, I still hold that there is a real idea in their daring move ; that, given the right sergeant, he could help you.

First, then, gentlemen, I congratulate you with all my heart on the use to which you have determined to put your life, and on the fact, surely awesome in its wonder, that the Lord Jesus Christ is graciously pleased to stoop to accept your offer of service. That is the central thing that matters. What He may choose to do with us, whether our lot lie in a big sphere, or in one less conspicuous ; and whether many, or, as in Christ's own case, few outward symptoms of success attend us, that is comparatively speaking unimportant. In either case, we are to be God's fellow-labourers : your hands are to touch His at the same task, His task. And, lest we mar it, lest we hinder Him instead of help, must we not toil with anxious diligence to catch some shadow of His own wholeheartedness in it, of His untiring eagerness, of His amazement of self-sacrifice. For we shall never preach, worth calling preaching, until our hearts run out to these fellow-men of ours, so gallantly facing their difficult lives, longing to set our backs against their backs and help them through, (for as Père Didon, the great preacher, has it, " your influence over a soul is conditioned by the depth of your love for it, in order to save it and bring a divine influence to bear upon it you must have a divine love for it ")—until, too, Christ is so big and wonderful to us that we can't keep Him to ourselves, must share Him with as many as will listen to us. Matters of technique and the grammar of preaching are all very well, and we shall come to these in time. But the first essential for our work, the one thing we must have, is a passion for Jesus Christ. And that is where some of us know that we are failing. We are too cool, too unconcerned, have not a sufficient sense of the bigness of the thing we have to offer ! How can we press Him upon others unless our own soul is exulting in Him :

how can we hope that they will learn of us
unless they feel that we ourselves know our
Lord intimately, and have the right to speak
of Him, that we ourselves have proved that
these wonderful promises of what He does
and is, are true, and that we hand them on
with confidence as what we know? As
old Bishop Wilson—whom Arnold preferred
grotesquely to À Kempis—has it, " to be
heartily in love with the truth one commends
is the great secret of becoming a good
preacher."

I beseech you in all your thinking about
preaching to begin there. Believe me, things
are not easy for one's own soul in the ministry,
and you must be upon your guard. Others
turn out of the rush and babble of the world
into God's temple, and the hush there acts
like a cool hand upon a fevered forehead :
but we live in the holy precincts always, and
they can lose some of their awesomeness
through long familiarity. Did they leave
the Holy of Holies with the dust of years
accumulating in it ? Or, if not, do you
imagine that the priest who dusted it day

after day felt the same awe as did the people standing afar off watching the High Priest entering it, once a year ? Others take the sacred vessels now and then into hands that tremble, but we finger them so constantly ! The Word of God can grow to be only a hunting-ground for texts ; and we can preach, meaning intensely every word we utter, yet in reality only lost for the moment like an actor in his part, or at least leaving it to the folk to live it out : for us, bless me, we have no time for that, but are already immersed, poor harried souls, in determining what we shall preach on next ; that is our bit of it. If you are not to drift into unconscious hypocrisy, or at least into using great words with little meaning, always a dangerous thing, live close to Jesus Christ.

It is a trying task that you are undertaking. Nearly always you will be tired, often you will be disappointed, sometimes you will grow querulous and peevish, or feel uneasily that you have run into a thing too big for you. Yet do not hesitate to give Christ what you have, pitiful offering though it look. For, you remember, He accepts us on the distinct understanding that He knows that without Him we can do, not fairly well though not enough, but just nothing at all. And you will find that He is an amazingly sufficient Master, with the oddest skill, even with blunt and most unserviceable looking weapons, and almost incredibly slow to blame.

I remember on the night of my induction at St. Matthew's, Glasgow, telling the people rashly enough that, though I could not preach well, I could promise to give them Sunday by Sunday the very best that there was in me, looking to the rush and bustle of each week ; and how months later, when I had forgotten all about it, going in one night to evening service, flushed and unhappy, with a very wretched sermon knocked together somehow now and then in hot and flustered days, half way up the pulpit stairs I came on Jesus Christ, saw Him quite plainly, heard Him saying, " And is this your very best this week," stood there, just where the steps bend yonder, and looked Him in the face, without fear, I remember, for His searching eyes were the kindest I have ever seen, thought the thing out there face to face with Him, and dared to answer that, in view of the full days, to me it seemed it almost was. And He said nothing, but He smiled. And I moved on and preached with a queer exultant elation, feeling that the wretched thing was passed.

Ours is a wonderful Master, and a glorious service ! Here am I, after five and twenty years of it, in days when matters like attendance have been ebbing, and with no signal encouragements in my own ministry to hearten me. And yet I tell you that I envy you coming into the firing line, with all your years of service still ahead.

In truth that business of the ebbing has been much exaggerated. Even yet religion is by far the most interesting subject in the world, and the people prove it by the way they flock to hear about it, even yet. Take any other theme you choose, politics let us say, and through a heated fortnight at an election time you can gather eager meetings. But let them continue, in scores and hundreds

of places in the cities, week in and week out
the whole year round, and what size would
they be in a twelve month ? But you—oh,
you will at times be grumpy over thin pews.
Watch yourself then; be sure that that is
really zeal for Christ, and not, as is much
more likely, merely hurt pride that stings
you. Never rail at a congregation because it
is small. It is not the fault of those who are
there. And in your deeper moods you will
stand gazing in amazement at the folk coming
back, sitting there looking hopefully toward
you, not yet discouraged, it appears, by
the sad persistent failures of the past, apparently still sure that God is going to break
through all our imperfections to them.

In any case, this ebbing is no new thing !
Always church-going has been a matter of
troughs and waves : and if to-day we are in
the trough, history promises that that means
that there is a wave coming up behind us :
that if our trough seems more than usually
deep, then it is a huge billow that is following,
that will roll in and crash far up on the beach.
After every war always there is a period of

stagnation, always followed by a glorious
reaction. Think it out! Marlborough's
campaigns, and then that utter deadness
when the French ambassador reported that
in England Christianity was obsolete. And
then? Why then, Wesley came and made
the doleful folk look foolish, as is usual in the
same world with God. The long Napoleonic
wars, and five and twenty years of spiritual
apathy thereafter. Yes, but followed by the
glory of Disruption days in Scotland, and the
amazing rush of the Tractarian movement
over England. And to-day, don't you imagine
that the hungry heart of man will always
credit that he can be satisfied with mere
material improvements! Footsore and tired
and disappointed, in time he will seek again
for something deeper, turn towards that Jesus
Christ whom now he thrusts impatiently aside.
And Christ in His forgiving way will forget the
insults, and will welcome him with eagerness.
It may take time ; it usually does. Perhaps,
if God will, I may see it ; but you fortunate
creatures almost surely will. What sign of
it, you ask ? Never a ripple on the waters !

Still only a glassy sea, where we rock idly,
make no progress, even drift back somewhat
with the tides. Yet, for trained eyes, already
there are darkening patches on the water
that tell us that the winds of God are nearer
than folk think. For is not the most striking
feature of our day the frank fashion in which
our leaders, admitting themselves baffled by
a time too difficult for them, are turning to
the church, begging its help, throwing the
burden of things on it and its preaching and
its pulpit as the one power that can pull us
through ? " We had not the requisite religious
force behind us," said Lloyd George, referring
to the failure of the Genoa Conference ; " and
it is for the church to supply that." " We
must look to the leaders of religion," said the
Premier of Japan, " for the carrying out by
their different countries of the Washington
Agreements." " No military preparedness,"
said Earl Haig, " no political expedient can
guarantee the kind of peace on which the
heart of the world is set. The Christian
religion, backed by a united Christendom and
a church as daring and heroic on spiritual

lines as the army has been on military lines, is the only hope of the world, and of the solution of the great problems with which the world is faced." When our leaders have reached that, the mass of men, footsore and disillusioned elsewhere, will soon be flocking back to it.

Gentlemen, nothing can stop a spiritual revival by and by, except one thing—that the men who ought to lead it, you, who will then be in the pulpits, may not be zealous and apt and big enough for such great times as are certainly coming, may not know our Lord well enough, or may not have the heart for such a glorious adventure, or may not have acquired the art of translating the gospel into the speech of your own time, may be lumbering half a generation in the rear, still muttering ancient, worn-out shibboleths. "Be sure they sleep not whom God needs," cries Browning in his gallant way. Yet they can, they often do. As that arresting person, Jacks of the Hibbert, puts it in a very pertinent question, " Emerson in a well-

known couplet assures us that the heedless
world has never lost one accent of the Holy
Ghost. How, I wonder, did Emerson find
that out ? " I wonder, too ! Gentlemen,
yours is a staggering responsibility. You
have been called to serve God in a great day
full of enormous probabilities. Don't let the
accent that the Holy Ghost would speak
through you to win back the careless world
die into silence because you did not know your
business, or through your half-heartedness
and bungling. Never has the office of
preaching been more momentous than it will
be in your time. Never has there been such
need to prepare for it with all our might.

And even before these great days come,
how splendid is your life-work. I know that
sometimes you will be inclined to agree
whole-heartedly with Manning when he said
despondently, though only to reject it, that
thirty years of preaching look like thirty
years of beating the air. But it is not so.
The weekly drip, drip, drip, wears in far
further than we think, does more, much more,
than we would credit. Never shall I forget

the shock when an experienced saint, far
further on than I am yet, told me long years
ago, when I was a mere gawky boy, " I have
a mighty gift for which to thank you. For
you have given me a new God. I never
realized before how lovable He is." And all
of us have letters, some of them indeed we
burned as being too sacred to be kept, that
we take out when things are "dowie," and,
reading the brave words of thanks, flush hot
with shame at our faint-heartedness. And
you will get them too, that, or a shy sentence,
or a pressure of the hand.

I know that you will sometimes feel that
the usefulness of the pulpit has thinned into
nothingness, or little more, as Carlyle often
thought. We hear, he says, " that the
Church is in danger : and truly so it is. Its
functions are becoming more and more
superseded. The true Church of England, at
this moment, lies in the Editors of its News-
papers." He of the " Daily Mail," I take
it, with his constant and soul-stirring call
to spirituality, and his brave contempt of
popularity and man's poor praise, the august

c

archbishop of that holy hierarchy ! I am the
son of an editor, and know the immense
power of the Press, yet—when you look back
at your old sermons you will, on occasion, be
amazed that you could ever have written such
silly nonsense. Be of good cheer, the biggest
men sometimes do that : Carlyle, for instance,
in that passage. Yet Robertson of Brighton,
of all people, in a whining mood, echoes
that sentiment, he whose world-wide and immeasurable influence makes his own words
seem preposterous. " I wish I did not hate
preaching so much, but the degradation of
being a Brighton preacher is almost intoler-
able. I do not depreciate spiritual work, I
hold it higher than secular : all I say and feel
is that by the change of times the pulpit has
lost its place. It does only part of that whole
that used to be done by it alone. Once it was
newspaper, schoolmaster, theological treatise,
a stimulant to good work, historical lecture,
metaphysics, etc., all in one. Now these are
partitioned out to different officers, and the
pulpit is no more the pulpit of three centuries
ago than the authority of the master of a

household is that of Abraham who was soldier, butcher, sacrificer, shepherd and emir in one person."

And a very good thing, too, say I, that we can nowadays cease from serving tables, and get on with our own job. Somehow it sticks in my mind that, just because Abraham was so immensely successful as the Father of the faithful, he was likely to be a bit unhandy as a butcher! And when a man in the pulpit strays into party politics it is humanity, it is a duty, to think vigorously of something else, and to keep telling yourself over and over that he will be far better when he returns home to his own sphere. Certainly what we see about us is a very rudimentary Christianity, and the pulpit must keep urging folk to work out in every sphere of life the implications of the faith with far greater thoroughness than most of us are doing. Yet, as Burke said, " politics and the pulpit are terms that have little agreement. Surely the Church is a place where one day's truce ought to be allowed to the dissensions and animosities of mankind. " I, at least for one, like Mr.

Cruger, his silent fellow-candidate, " say ditto
to Mr. Burke." We have no right to claim
Christ exclusively for any one political party,
though every Christian man will join that one
that seems to him nearest to Christ's mind.
On principles, we Christian people ought to
be agreed. But on the wisdom, or the reverse,
of any particular endeavour to work out these
principles, every Christian man must be
allowed to exercise his own judgment, and
follow his own conscience, face to face with
Christ. And it is seldom that a man has the
right to lay it down in the pulpit that on a
debatable question of the day he has the mind
of Christ, and that whoso differs from him
parts with the Master. It is, I submit, the
function of the preacher, not to cover every
province of life with minute rules saying, in
each circumstance, this is what you ought to
do, and that is what you must avoid; but to
get people so in love with the principles of
Christ that when they go back, each to
his own sphere, whether that sphere be
trade, or politics, or anything else, they will
endeavour, there where they live, in that

with which they have to do, to work them out.

Gentlemen, stick to your own job. For there never was more need of it than now, when people are so rushed and jostled that God almost inevitably fades from their bustled minds, when these services of ours come to many as almost the only reminder of the unseen things, like those sudden glimpses from the heart of Edinburgh of the blue sea and the far hills and the islands laughing in the sunshine, and then the houses shut it out again, but for a little we remember : or like the flower that Alexander Smith chanced on, that day on a hot Glasgow pavement, and it rushed in on him, so busy and so rigorously imprisoned, that all around the city there was summer, and for a while he saw it all, the glory of the cornfields, and the witchery of flowers, and the long, rolling moors of heather ; and his tired heart felt cooler. They called our Lord the " Word of God." And in your tiny way you also are to be a word of God, almost the only one that will get through the noise and crowding of their bustled lives to some hearts desperately needing it.

I know that we are told that in an age of books there is small need of gathering together. When one has but to stretch out his hand, and can at once be sitting at the feet of the noblest preachers of all time, why should one turn aside from them to listen to our fumbling amateurish ineffectiveness? That sounds quite reasonable.   And yet is it?

For one thing, the number of those who really read such books is very small.   And further, there is a queer something about a fellow-man there visibly addressing one.   Your student of French, much though he can learn from books, must go to France to catch the real accent of the thing from living voices; can learn more, in many ways, from a mere child than from the most learned of tomes.   So, somehow, even an ineffective speaker can often do more for us in some respects than can the best of books.   Hence the University, and not simply the library; the political campaign, and not merely the Press; the sermon, and not only a half-hour of quiet reading in the home.

I know that doleful people tell us that

wireless is a portent, a sure prophecy that the
old style of things is gone, and that Church
services are the dwindling survivals of a bygone
age, lessening pools left high up on the drying
beach by a sea that will have no returning
tide. Perhaps. But human nature rarely
changes ; and probably on to the end, when
people feel deeply or are moved in any way,
they will still tend to herd together, as they
always have done in the past. Somehow the
feel of these other shoulders touching ours as
they, too, swing on their way to the same far
goals, heartens and helps us not a little. Keats,
indeed, who did not like parsons, looks
forward hopefully, in one of his letters, to a
time when they will be so extinct that, coming
on a description of them in some learned
volume, people will no more believe in such
monstrosities than we do in the phœnix.
But that time, at least, is not yet.

In any case, yours is to be an interesting
life. You are to move about among a people
as Christ's representative, with endless little
opportunities of helpfulness made for you,
your presence often welcomed as a proof that

God has not forgotten. That, in itself, is a wonderful thing. I remember one day visiting in Glasgow. Ah ! those cruel Glasgow stairs ! I am no mystic ; have had only two visions in my life. I have already told you one, here is the other, and so an end of that. One day visiting, I turned in dog-tired about ten at night to yet another stair, but I paused at the foot, and " I will go to-morrow," I determined, and was turning back when Someone passed me, and went up. And I knew who it was ! Yes ! Yes ! quite so, not a doubt of it ! Just tired nerves, as you say. But I knew who it was, heard Him say, " Well, if you won't go, then I must go myself " ; saw indeed only a dim greyness of mounting shoulders, dreadfully tired shoulders. But I knew Who it was, flushed to my soul, and ran up after Him, and Christ and I went in together. And for a while that kept it in my mind that we are meant to bring Christ with us when we visit, to make people have the happy feeling that He, too, is there—for a while, for a while !

But, in the main, it will be through the

services you can do most for them. And
every part of each of them can be an avenue
along which God's grace can and will sweep
in, if only we don't fumble, don't obscure it,
by our bungling.

The Sacraments! Gentlemen, have you
realized that one day you will have to stand
in Christ's place at His table, will be His hand
wherewith He gives needy souls that bread
that is His body. " Prayer time," says Faber,
is " God's punishment time." It is then that
our disloyalties come home to roost. But I
don't know that our sins ever look so ghastly
as they do at Christ's table, when we seem to
soil the very vessels with our touch, and are
afraid that we may block the rush of God's
grace to His people.

There is something hauntingly impressive
about our Scottish communions. Few Scots
ever feel anywhere else just that same thrill,
that hush of spirit, that sense that the big
things that matter are very real and very near,
that they are face to face with very God. It
is with held breath and listening hearts that
they wait in that brooding silence. And yet

I am not certain that we always catch what seems to me, at least, to be the fitting mood for sitting down with Christ.

Fearful of intruding where we have no right, are we not apt to be too introspective, and too self-absorbed, to carry on our self-examination even in Christ's presence, when we ought to be humbly and wonderingly taking at His hand ? No doubt the services of Preparation are not now attended as they used to be, and preparation and realization have to be crowded into one full hour. Yet, surely, the Communion Sermon ought to treat of the free gospel, and the open door, of the Master seeking for us everywhere, of eager hands laid upon us and drawing us in, and setting us in our own place prepared for us with loving care, and heaping lavish benefits upon us, of Christ making us feel that it would not have been the same to Him at all, if we had stayed away.

May I add this, as my own personal opinion, for what it is worth. Little though he suspects it, fiercely indeed though he would resent the imputation as a grotesque paradox, the average Scot is an abnormally High Churchman in his own way. And he proves it by the sparing use that he makes of the Sacraments, so sparing that Roman Catholics and Anglicans gaze at him in astonishment. Yet he, on his side, looks somewhat askance at people who find it possible to use as part of their daily spiritual food what is, to him, a thing so awesome and tremendous that he employs it only as his last line of defence, as the reserves that he throws in to turn the tide of battle, as a trumpet-call that fires his soul again. They tell me that some feel we celebrate Communion far too seldom. If that be so, then we should have some churches with very frequent celebration to meet such people's needs. But for myself, (like draws to like), I scarcely ever hear expression given to that view except from men brought up in English schools, who have, perhaps, lost touch a little with the national mood. At all events, " No," said Rainy, agreeing with my preference for thin sown communion seasons ; " I find that twice a year, the old custom with us, makes it for most of us much

more of an event, a new beginning, a real
rallying-point." Certainly I, who in various
congregations have seen most ways of it, set
it down as my opinion that for most Scots
people that is so.

Of the conducting of an ordinary service
there is so much that one might say. The
glow of the whole, for example, is dependent
in quite a remarkable degree upon the choice
of the Praise. How a poor hymn can spoil
things! How a ranting tune, or insincere
or over-emphasized words, can jar and
stumble! For Scottish congregations here
is a fact worth pondering. Out at the front
I used often to allow the men to choose the
praise. It was rarely they asked for a hymn.
Much oftener they plumped for psalms and
paraphrases. And no wonder! For there
are a body and soul about the best of these,
and the old tunes to which they are wedded,
modern hymns and modern music all too often
lack. Whether a Service ought to be a unity,
in the sense that Praise and Scripture and
indeed everything should all match with
exactness, is a moot point. Upon the whole,

I would say, No. There must be no noisy
clash. But you are faced by many lives,
some grey, some sunny, and there ought to be
something in the Father's House for all His
children.

Or take the reading of the Scriptures,
which ought always to be set full in the
centre of the service, as the climax to the
whole, where the light falls directly on
it. Compared to it, our own poor bits
of sermons are a very trivial affair, a
mere footnote in small print, nothing more!
If they forget that, usually it deserves it.
And who cares about that, so long as their
minds are haunted by the depth and cadences
and glory of our Lord's own perfect words.
A well-known minister, whose books have a
wide circulation, told me once that all the
spiritual happenings in his notable ministries
have come, not through his sermons, but
through the reading of the Scriptures, for
which he prepares himself with absorbed care.
And surely that is credible enough. For what
words of yours or mine are so likely to grip
and move and win folks as, say, the story

of the Prodigal, which I protest that I have never yet read in public without that sudden something rising up chokingly in my throat. And, since we are all of one kin, no doubt in the pews they are feeling that too. Those of you who can read Scripture well, not oratorically—that is hateful—but simply, reverently, feeling it themselves, lost in it, can be quite sure that they will always reach some hearts. While, on the other hand, Wesley once in the Episcopal Chapel in Aberdeen could hear only one word of the first lesson, and no more in the second ; and, with an adroit thrust at the perfectly un-merited reputation of the folk of that fine city for extra carefulness about finance, set down in his Journal that night that he wondered they did not see that it would be more profit-able to them " to pay the man to keep quiet ! "

Or Prayer, a theme sufficient in itself for a long course of lectures. What a tremendous, a cruel, weight of responsibility our type of service throws on us through that ! Perhaps in time we may become partly liturgical.

That certainly would be a real help to some minds, both in the pulpit and in the pews. For as things are, unless a man is careful, the congregation are too much at the mercy of his mood. Yet there are facts that tell the other way. In my first charge in Liverpool a large proportion of the members were ex-Anglicans, and nearly always what attracted them was what they called the free prayer, to them a continual delight. Even the glorious Prayer Book had grown trite to them, it seemed. And indeed liturgies, I fear, would not greatly help me, who find it difficult at times to repeat even the Lord's Prayer, putting any meaning into the great words, which, through familiarity, are apt to slip through my unarrested mind, much like a knotless thread that leaves nothing behind.

And there is this real difficulty that the very beauty of a prayer may keep one from praying. The mind is lost in admiring the perfection of the English, or the loveliness of the thought, is listening, agreeing, commending, but not praying. So I have found. And

Dr. Hastings, of the Dictionaries, used to find that too.

Once on a time I used to insert into each service a little collect, or the like, which I had let the people know was never my own, but always taken from some master of devotion. But I was disappointed to discover that the congregation did not seem to be impressed by them, as my mind was. Though once a good soul, who had been gravely annoyed that I had given a course of lectures in the class on the chief prophets of the other faiths, had been a little troublesome about it, came to me all gratitude for one brief prayer which had, he said, brought God so near that he had caught his breath. " Yes," I replied, " I can well believe that. That was a prayer of Muhammad ! " There is seldom need to lose one's temper. For an ironic humour runs through life that usually gives one back one's own—in time.

But, as things are, what a burden it is we must carry. To pray at all, Coleridge used to say, is the highest and hardest office of the human mind. But to try to gather up and present the worship, the petitions, the confession, the thanksgiving—and all the great saints lay tremendous stress on that, thanksgiving is the highest type of prayer—all the ache and sobbing and desire of a whole body of needy souls, to stagger to God on their behalf, and state for them their separate cases in their several names, " desperate tides of the whole great world's anguish, forced through the channels of a single heart " —what an unthinkable task ! To me it is amazing it is carried through even as worthily as it is. Denney, indeed, once said to me that in church up and down the land he was rarely disappointed with the sermon, but as rarely satisfied with the devotions. And I note that the experts tend to agree with him. I am not sure I do. A sermon, even in Scotland, can be fairly dull and boring to one in the pews : so one discovers when one happens to stray there. But almost always the prayers move and help. At all events it is impossible to exaggerate the importance of that portion of our work, or to overdo one's preparation for it. Tell me, I once asked a

D

great business man in Glasgow, which is the
bit of the service that you laymen find most
helpful. And without hesitation he replied,
" there is no manner of doubt concerning that
—the intercessory prayer." Often, so he
explained, we people come to church too
tired to follow a discourse closely. The mind
is fagged and loses grip at times, thoughts
wander, other things intrude. But, if the
intercession have some width and amplitude
and particularity in it, suddenly hearing its
own exact case stated, the soul, however
weary, starts awake, and makes a clutch at
God, feeling Him at its side. To-day, he
instanced, you happened to pray for those
expecting letters, and they never come.
Quite certainly some half a dozen suddenly
grew comforted, feeling that God had not
forgotten, that He knew about their trouble,
and had given them a promise He would
surely see to it.

Certainly public prayer is a grave danger
for a minister. It is so easy to say what we
know is the proper thing to say, even when
it tinkles emptily in our mind. And, as

Mr. Birrell has it, that must be a dreadful moment when a man has the feeling he is praying well. Yet even that is possible. Steep your minds, gentlemen, in the great classics of devotion. They will not only save you from unseemliness of phrasing, and from insincerity of thought; but, until you do, you can have no idea what a marvellous thing prayer is, how intimate it can become, how near God one can draw, what a tremendous power it can exert. And you have no right to defraud your people of what you could give them with a little trouble.

For my part, I am not helped most by set and rotund phrases, exquisite though these may be. Anything formal is to me a barrier. I well remember worshipping as a boy in Westminster Abbey, much moved by the beauty of the service in that noble House of God, with the great dead around one, and with endless memories haunting the mind, till the soul bowed in reverence before the Almighty God Who was, and Who is, and Who is to come. Yet the next Sunday in a tiny country church in Perthshire, miles from anywhere, in a bare little place with only a few shepherds and their dogs scattered thinly here and there, the birches tapping on the open windows, through which there came the lapping of the loch—our only organ—the hot sun filling one's nostrils with a homely smell of varnish—oh, quite unseemly, as you say —and yet, and yet, there I felt God far closer, and a God much dearer and more lovable at that. The Heavenly Father seemed among us, with a few bairns of His gathered close to His knees, and His arms were fairly round us. So, for me, prayer is nearest the ideal when simple, short (I cannot really pray for more than a few minutes, often not more than five when someone else is leading), scrupulously honest, spoken not to One far away but there, not a pleading that God would be gracious, but an assuming that He is, a childie talking humbly and yet confidently to his Father, sure of His interest and love.

I am aware, of course, that, as Matthew Henry put it, prayer is like the boatman's hook, meant, not to draw the shore to the boat, but the boat to the shore; that often we have to chafe our cold souls into a glow, to gain the spirit of expectancy which will receive God's answers. And yet is there not something in old, dry John Selden's feeling ? " If a man hath a voluble tongue, we say, ' he hath the gift of prayer.' His gift is to pray long, that I see. But does he pray better ? Prayer should be short, without giving God Almighty reasons why He should grant this or that. He knows best what is good for us. If your boy should ask a suit of clothes, and give reasons, ' otherwise he cannot wait upon you, he cannot go abroad but he will discredit you,' would you endure it ? You know it better than he : let him ask a suit of clothes."

At all events, here is a useful rule. " Herbert," says Baxter, " speaks to God like a man who really believeth in God, and whose business in the world is most with God."

But this lectureship deals in the main with Preaching. And wisely. For, as the Catechism has it, " it is especially the preaching of the Word which the Spirit of God makes an effectual means of convincing and converting

sinners, and of building them up in holiness
and comfort through faith unto salvation."

We Presbyterians are often twitted upon
the importance we give to the sermon. And
indeed that can be overdone. Some of us
need to learn to worship. And yet the weight
that we lean upon preaching is not merely the
substituting of an intellectual interest for real
religion. (And, mind you, it is not a little
thing that in Scotland we can claim that
preaching *is* an intellectual interest). It is an
instinct bidding us line the road that Christ
has always travelled, to keep looking in the
direction from which He has always come.
For you may talk how you will about beauty
and art and music, and their spiritual appeal.
And they are all necessary. And our service
is lopsided and inadequate, if even one is
missing. But always it has been through
preaching that revivals have come : always
by preaching that the Spirit has made the
tired Church young again. No bustle of
energy can do it, no whirring of machinery,
sending a gale into our tired faces, no endless
and elaborate organisation, no, and no glory of

art. For some of us that can easily become a dangerous thing, ending in a mere ephemeral gush of emotion that evaporates without result, but which creates the pleasant feeling in us that something is going on, as, of course, in its own way, a sermon too can do, ending no less futilely. Still, if history is any guide, if you are to win back the world for God, it will far likeliest be through preaching. And you must lay the main stress there. Always it is the preacher, the prophet, who fires men's souls, and brings in a new era.

In part no doubt you may have to adopt new methods. Every age must. For one thing it looks as if you would have to take to the streets, if you have any aptitude for that. I have not. And I would rigorously exclude those who have failed. The work is by far too important to be jeopardized by bunglers. Very carefully should the church choose those who are to state its case to the vast mass outside it in our land. " I preached on the quay at Kingswood, and near King's Square," says Wesley far on in his life ; " to this day field preaching is a cross to me. But I know my commission, and see no other way of preaching the gospel to every creature." If you have any of the powers of a good parliamentary candidate ; if you are cool, and ready, and quick with a reply, and have some popular gifts, you might do splendid service in the open air.

Every one will admit that one of the most marked features in recent political life is the way in which the Labour Party has stormed Glasgow. Whether we like it or do not, there the fact is. Listen, then, to this little story. Years ago in that great hive I was hurrying to a meeting in a distant part of the city one Sunday morning before the cars began, and noticed what was then quite a new thing, the pavements chalked at intervals with invitations to a hall. I stopped a policeman, and asked what it meant. " These are Socialists," he said ; " and since very early morning they have been out and about, inviting the whole universe to a little place that will hold scarcely anyone. Believe me, sir, I disagree with them, but men, so much in earnest as they are, are sure one day to sweep the city. What can hold them ? What can keep them down ? " And then he added, " Why are you ministers not out, and at it too ? You have a case far better and more glorious. If you would only work for it as these men do for theirs, why, you would sweep the world." I have often, since then, thought of my unknown policeman and his prophecies. One of them has come true. And, if we took him at his word, would not the other also ?

But wherever you are to exercise it, and in the main it will be in your churches, what an office it is to which you have set your hands ! " I know not," wrote John Cairns to Sir William Hamilton, his teacher ; " what lives may lie before me, but on to the ending end of them I shall bear your mark upon me." In measure that is true, for good or evil, dreadfully true, of all ministers and their congregations. Have you ever seen a sculptor in his studio—how, when he is at work upon the clay, he toils earnestly but quickly ? For at the worst a swift turn of thumb and finger can put right a blunder. But watch him now, his whole soul in his eyes, how tense and careful, scarcely breathing. Ah ! he is working on the lasting marble now, where a slip were fatal. But your material is immortal souls ! The solid earth will pass and be forgotten like the shadows blown along the hills and gone, but they will still remain as real as ever, and with your mark still upon them.

Or think of what it is you are to handle. " Hold," cried Malan to old Rabbi Duncan, and the words ran through him like a shock of electricity; " hold, you have got the Word of God in your mouth." And so have we : the *Word of God*, and yet how easily, how impudently, we too often handle it, passing our light opinions on it, chattering round about it, until we fill in our time, not really studying it, or using it, but rather making it a peg on which we hang our own poor shallow notions !

Remember, too, the glorious succession in which you are in your turn to stand. For it is not for nothing that the ministry is so honoured in Scotland ! " I have drawn much

closer to your faith," Lord Morley once said
to me, " and that partly through what I have
seen in Scotland, for here your people, and
especially your ministers, seem much nearer
to the reality of things than they appear to
me at least elsewhere." The Scottish Church
has had its glaring faults, yet the people
believe in it, as well they may. Because it
is the church, through its ministry, that has
won for them what they most prize; that
ministry that has again and again stood
between them and danger, and that often has
been the only voice to rally them when kings
were tyrants, and the nobles did not care! In
dark days it has never broken, persecuted it
has never quailed, has time and again boldly
led the way through a long, black, starless
midnight out into a fuller day. In your time
also there will be problems to face and
difficulties to be met, and you must be
worthy of the traditions of the Service.

Once at the front they spilt us out of motor
lorries on the darkest and wettest night I
ever saw. And in the morning we discovered
that we were on High Wood Battlefield, on

the exact spot where a year before the
battalion had been wiped out in a superb
charge. We spent the forenoon wandering
among the crosses yonder, some of them white,
our own, some of them German grey; noted
with pride how unbelievably far our lads had
won, and with warm gratitude that above
two of them deep in their lines a generous
enemy had written the Battalion, and the
words, " A very gallant Scot "—I think they
were. And that afternoon we moved on.
The next day was a Sunday, and I knew that
we were to be thrown into the Hindenburg
line—knew, too, that the men knew that I
knew : and there I preached to them on
" Seeing we are compassed about with so great
a cloud of witnesses, . . . let us too, run " :
spoke of the crosses we had seen, our crosses,
cried to them that we dared not be false to
the tartan that had won such glory, to the
lads, our lads, who had died for us, aye or to
Jesus Christ our wonderful Saviour. And
that day here and there a boy would come up
shyly, " Thank you, padre," he would say, " I
promise you that I will not be false to our

dead, or to Jesus Christ ; " and gloriously they proved it true. We too have great traditions, and you also must walk worthy of them.

Aye, and you can. Do you remember how when Elijah, his great master, was taken away, Elisha, a much plainer and more ordinary man, snatched up the garment that had fallen from him, stood by the Jordan, smote it, crying " Where is the God of Elijah ? " And he found He was still there. And you too will learn that the old power our fathers knew is still here if you care to use it ; and that God is still as much alive and real as in the biggest moments of the past.

Elijah's garment ! It is far more wonderful than that ! For is there not Another with a seamless robe, which poor souls touched, and new power came to them ? And He has gifted that to you, promises you that the works that He did you shall do also. Yes, He says, till we look up wonderingly at Him, " and even greater than Mine " ; pledges Himself that never will His folk and you gather together but He will be there among you—always you can count on that, He says—that never will you preach but tired hearts will be cheered, and crooked lives be straightened, and souls found and helped. I promise it, He says. And I believe it, literally.

Here is a Master worth the serving, and a life-work worthy of our very best! John Brown declared that the reason why vastly superior numbers broke before him was, themselves being witnesses, that " they lacked a cause." We, thank God, have a cause to live for, and a dream to inspire us, and a power to bring us through, if only we will work for it, follow it, use it !

There are a thousand things that we should touch upon, a hundred aptitudes that we must try to learn, and every one of them will help us, and none of them dare we neglect. To do so were to shut ourselves into a narrow sphere, and to limit our influence. But first of all, and over all, and most of all, really to preach must we not have a thrilling feeling of the greatness of our office, and the glory of the Master, and the splendour of our task ?

Has something of that reached you, as a new pride in my uniform swept over me that dark night at Bailleul, as my companion still droned on, a grim determination that I also, please God, would be worthy of it, that I too would do what men frail as myself had done ? Has the thrill and the glory of it touched your mind again ? If not, alas for your poor stupid sergeant, clumsier than mine, and alas for you !

PREACHING resembles music in this respect
that for a real success three things are required
—a theme worth hearing, a sufficient instrument, and a master whose deft touch can draw
from both what his soul finds in them. As
preachers we possess the needed theme, far and
away the most heart-gripping and inspiring in
the world. What a reflection on us bunglers
it is that we have so mishandled the chivalry
and glory of that exciting, valorous, thrilling
tale of Jesus Christ, that we are told these
days that people are so thoroughly bored by
such a very dull and stale affair as we have
made of it that twenty minutes' talk about it
is fully as much as they can stand, and anything more really an infliction through which
they can only yawn and fidget miserably—the
very people who will spend hours upon hours
at a more or less silly opera, or over some
transient tale ! With such a subject we ought
to have swept the world.

And we have a marvellous instrument, out of tune a bit, so all the experts are agreed, and not entirely dependable ; yet even as it is the greatest of all God's creations, so far as we know. For we play on the living, throbbing hearts and minds and wills of men and women ; can draw out such marvellous stops ! Watch a master, how inevitably he secures response from it to his own every mood. A touch on this, and all the sobbing sorrow of many experiences answers you ; or a quick finger upon that, and the brave hearts are ringing out their exultation, or their valiant daring of defiance—a glorious instrument which, even for fumbling hands, it is a sheer delight to play, and feel it giving answering expression to our inmost thoughts. But if we had sufficient art and skill and knowledge, what could we not do with it ?

I once had an impressive experience sitting on the seat behind the pulpit in St. George's, Edinburgh, when Whyte was preaching to the great packed church. I could not see his face, yet I could follow with exactness all the ever-shifting play of sunshine and shadow

E

that kept passing over it. Apparently he frowned, for all these listening faces darkened. And then his must have cleared, for all these others suddenly lit up. There they were, so mastered, so absorbed, so lost in the sermon, so one with him, that, all unconsciously, they acted as a perfect mirror of his every mood.

If nothing much is happening in our case, and the services dribble on dully enough to their slow tame end, it is wise to look for the reason of that, not in some cantankerous perversity in other folk, that desperate explanation upon which our wounded pride is apt to fasten greedily, but in some defect in ourselves. Do you remember Johnson upon Savage? " Though he paid due deference to the suffrages of mankind when they were given in his favour, he did not suffer his esteem of himself to depend on others, nor found anything sacred in the voice of the people, when they were inclined to censure him. He then readily showed the folly of expecting that the public should judge right, observed how slowly poetical merit had often forced its way into the world ; he contented

himself with the applause of men of judgment,
and was somewhat disposed to exclude all
those from the character of men of judgment
who did not applaud him." That is a bit of
acute psychology we had better remember.

No doubt the people are not infallible. Jesus
Christ lost His crowd. They tired of Him,
they shrugged their shoulders, they criticized,
they flocked elsewhere. And we have known
consummate preachers spending themselves on
a handful thinly sown about the pews ; while,
round the corner, crowds stood gaping after
some far smaller man, with a comparatively
ordinary message. As an Australian padre
put it to me once in Glasgow, his eyes wide
with astonishment, " I have just had an
unbelievable experience, have heard far and
away the finest sermon I can ever hear
preached to the smallest congregation I can
ever see. What does it mean ? " It meant
of course that this is a queer world where odd
things sometimes happen.

Still, if nothing comes of it in our own case,
we shall be fairly safe in taking it for granted
that the fault lies with ourselves, that there

is something in us inefficient or disturbing, which we had better try to find, and to right, if we can.

As to popularity, let nobody pretend to despise that. In nine cases out of ten it is not altogether honest : and in at least three of the nine has in it a touch of sour grapes ! Certainly in itself popularity proves nothing, one way or the other. Shakespeare in some moods considered it as the hall-mark of an entirely unoriginal mind, that tramps along flat-footedly with the crowd. " Thou art a blessed fellow," as Prince Hal has it, " to think as every man thinks : never a man's thoughts in the nation keeps the roadway better than thine ! " And Shakespeare obviously did not think highly of the crowd, or the crowd's judgments. And Goethe's prescription for popularity is frankly contemptuous. " The Public," he says, " is a great baby, you must give it what it wants, or it will cry." While Carlyle is still more severe, " He preaches it aloud," he says, " and rushes courageously forth with it—if there is a multitude huzzaing at his back : yet ever keeps looking over his shoulder, and the instant the huzzaing languishes, he too stops short."

All of which may be true enough in certain cases. Yet there are instances where popularity means nothing more or less than that a man knows his business, and the Gospel of Christ, and the human heart, and how to apply that one to that other. Are we not here to commend Christ to the world? And if we are not touching it, are we not so far failing, for some reason, bad perhaps, or perhaps good, still failing.

Though, indeed, popularity is an elusive thing that seems to flutter here and there, much like a butterfly that, hovering and hesitating, settles, or does not, but flits on and lights somewhere else for no discernible reason. At least many of those who have held their fellows in the hollow of their hand did so while flagrantly breaking all the accepted rules, or some of the most fundamental of them. Ambrose Shepherd, that fine preacher, had a queue winding far down the street for years and years. " Yes," he said to me with a laugh, "and it is easily explained, two-thirds of them have never heard a sermon of mine! And a good thing, too! For if they had, they would never have come back." A ridiculous reason, of course! And yet there was just this touch of truth in it that he was really ill heard by the mass of folk, a fact which would have been to you or me just fatal, but to him, somehow, it did not matter. Why?

Or take the classic case of Chalmers and the tumult of enthusiasm he created everywhere, he who seemed to have an impossible handicap against him, with his lumpish figure, his dull heavy face, and leaden eyes, his drawling voice and execrable accent, his close reading of his manuscript, his uncouth gestures, his huge sermons—turgid stuff often, too, at that, judged by our standards now— everything seemed against him. Yet somehow people were content to wait till he slowly caught fire ; and then he fascinated, mastered, awed them. You remember how like one man they leaned forward, as the mighty paragraph gathered itself and rolled in till it crashed in some tremendous phrase : at

which there came a universal sigh, and then
once more that eager leaning forward, and
again that sigh. There are many witnesses
to that. You cannot really explain popularity
in preaching : you cannot lay down rules for
what in essence is a queer, unaccountable,
capricious thing. It comes, or else it doesn't,
that is all that one can say. It seems largely
to depend on that odd indefinable thing
called personality, which one has or has not.
Apparently in the last resort it is not what
one says, or even how one says it, it is what
one is that gives the power. Though that
opens the question of the common yet most
puzzling fact that one can crowd out a church
here, and yet in one's next sphere may miss fire
altogether ; not to speak of such notorious
cases as Savonarola's who, at the moment that
a mere pulpiteer, a thing of pretty phrases and
rhetorical tricks, had the whole city flocking
after him, reduced an enormous congregation
to less than twenty-five, all told, including
children, and yet eight years later in that
same city was sweeping the crowds as the
winds bend the corn, and setting half Europe

on fire.   It is a puzzling business.   Here too
" the whole world stands at ' why.' "

And yet do you recall the story of Guthrie of
Fenwick, that most lovable of souls, that
prince of preachers, to whose little moorland
kirk people flocked from all directions, from
impossible distances, and always the Spirit of
God was manifestly in their midst, until they
silenced his wonderful voice, and forced in on
his folk a dull Episcopalian curate with no
food for their souls, though the life of the
ousted man was spared.   And how, unsoured,
he used to worship among his old congregation
—in itself a bonnie touch : and how one
day as, trailing home discontentedly, they
complained bitterly of the poverty of the
preaching, he dissented, maintained that it
was an excellent sermon, and sitting down
there on the heather preached it again to
them, but now with what a difference, to
hearts touched, troubled, comforted, moved,
set on fire—the same, and yet a thousand
miles away from it, because of that queer
indescribable something that unconsciously
he added.

How can we gain that, you and I ? Nobody can tell you. Perhaps as clear a pointer toward it as any you can find is this from Gladstone after a European tour. Comparing Italian to English preachers, and greatly preferring the former, he proceeds: " The preacher bears an awful message. Such messengers, if sent with authority, are too much identified with, and possessed by, that which they carry, to view it objectively during its delivery. It absorbs their very being, and all its energies : they *are* their message, and they see nothing extrinsic to themselves except those to whose hearts they desire to bring it." That is arresting testimony from the mouth of one who swayed his fellows as few men ever did. And this the more, seeing that Caird, that mighty pulpit orator, corroborates it almost line for line. Undoubtedly we never really preach till we are lost in, are, our message. But for some of us blunderers there is this difficulty that it is just when that happens, when we are carried away out of ourselves, and forget everything but our theme and our desire to press it on those listening that we are aptest to lose touch with them for some physical reason, to speak too rapidly, or to lower the voice, or somehow to become less audible. And yet the moment you remember that and pull yourself up to correct it, the divine afflatus vanishes, and you flutter earthwards on a broken wing. We have come out of our message to think about our voice or some such secondary thing, are no longer identified with it, possessed by it, lost in it.

Perhaps the most that one can do to attain a hold upon his fellows is to give one's best, to be, not surly as the natural man is apt to be, but grateful for criticism as to manner and methods, and with diligence to try at least to tame one's faults, praying here also that prayer of Euripides they found among his papers after his death: " Omnipotent God, send light unto men, that they may know whence their evils come, and learn how to avoid them." But, after all is said and done, popularity in preaching seems a very obvious proof of the Shakespearean saw, " some are born great, some achieve greatness, and some have greatness thrust upon them," with this blunt addendum, that the vast majority never can and never do reach it at all.

But to press on to deeper things. For, after all, there is truth in that saying of Ian Maclaren, himself accustomed to face crowded aisles, that numbers have nothing to do with spiritual things. "Believe me," he used to cry to us in a vexed way, "Christianity had already started to decline when in the Book of the Acts they were vulgar enough to begin to count the numbers of those being saved." To talk wistfully round and about that real success that we all covet (else what are we doing in the ministry?), that gift of helpfulness, that skilled touch upon souls, that faculty of making people see God to be so lovable that their hearts break away to Him, and Christ so real and near and sufficient that they rise up with a new hope, and face their difficulties no longer afraid, that power of bringing Him and them together face to face. As for the other matter, it must come or go as the gods will, but this we must have : and our whole hearts dream of it, search for it, strain toward it.

And how can we get nearer to it, you and I ?

We must start deep enough; begin sufficiently far back, not with the text and talk about heads and divisions and the like, but with ourselves. For, in this profound sense also, it is true that the real secret of successful preaching lies largely in one's personality. " It is not what I have or what I do, it is what I am that is my kingdom," says Carlyle. Here at least it is likely to be through that one will attain and reach it.

Think it out, and you will see that it must be so. You cannot describe Christianity from without, any more than from that angle you can see the meaning of a stained glass window. And that unmistakable touch of intimacy, that sense that this is first-hand knowledge, to which experienced souls always respond, seems possible only in one who has himself penetrated from the outer courts far into the holier places.

Other things one can learn by reading about them. So at least it is assumed, though, perhaps, Keats was right when he thought not. "Nothing ever becomes real till it is experienced. Even a proverb is no proverb to you till your life has illustrated it. Axioms in philosophy are not axioms till they are proved upon our pulses. We read fine things, but never feel them to the full until we have gone the same steps as the authors." At all events spiritual things can be learned only by being them. As Porphyry says, speaking of this high region, "Like is known only to like, and the condition of all knowledge is that the subject should become like the object." And the object of our thought and speech is God. Only the pure in heart can see Him, or describe Him with some adequacy.

It is of course true that we are not back in Old Testament times, that a man's standing with God cannot be reckoned by his success, even although that be in helping souls. Let us remember that. For no heresy ever really dies out of the world. Many an one who jeers at the crude notion of judging one's spiritual condition by the size of one's herds, can think God has forgotten him, if his young communicants be few.

Yet what we are, tells on our preaching constantly, and makes an enormous difference. Take an illustration. You remember the tremendous page in Amiel when he declares that every life is a sermon continually being preached to others, an endless propaganda tending to change them into one's own likeness, a lighthouse casting its beams over the tumbling waters, and guiding our fellow men, if not into the haven, then upon the rocks. We ministers can easily be guilty of that last, and in this way. You will agree that, in so far as we are not corrected by others, we all tend to create a god in our own image : that if, for example, we are living complacently in ways we know to be unworthy, that really means that because we easily forgive ourselves, we assume that God too is immorally indifferent to it and will let us off, is not going to make a fuss about it, but will smuggle us through somehow. That is to say, our god is not the Christian God ; and all unconsciously to us that other face will keep looking, as from a window, out of our sermons and views. We cannot hide it. It will show inevitably. But the power of the pulpit is tremendous: and in so far as we are influencing them, the congregation tends to think of God as we do, and we have discovered that we picture Him in our own likeness. Therefore, more or less, it is our shadow, cast enormously across their minds they see, a god blurred and distorted by our weaknesses and sins. Well might Keble, writing to a man the evening before his ordination, tell him that " his first duty would always be to keep himself in order." For we preach through our personality.

That of course tells both ways. I was once honoured to be the colleague of one of the biggest souls in Scotland. He was little known, for his fame was purely local. Yet he was a man of fascinating nature, big, human, humorous, of notable mental gifts, and of an arresting saintliness and strength of character—Alexander Cumming, of Forfar. He had passed through storms and difficulties in his day; but when I knew him in old age, the whole town, for all the coolness of its mental climate, looked up to him in reverence. As the tall, stooping, venerable figure moved

about the streets, pausing to pet a bairn, or
slipping up a close on yet another of the
endless little kindnesses with which he crowded
his happy days, faces everywhere lit up at
the sight of him ; and people, their voices
suddenly grown softer, became kindlier in
conversation when he hove in sight. So he
passed to and fro, a kind of benediction to
us all, as if God's own hand had been laid
in tenderness upon us. I well remember how
one of the chief men in the place, strong,
self-reliant, and with many admirable qualities, but not one whom you would have
thought could be easily touched, looked after
him one day. " Often I pull myself together
with this thought," he said, " that if I threw
away my life, I think that I could bear my
punishment without whining, but, but "—and
the man's voice sagged a little—" I could
not face the pain in Mr. Cumming's eyes."
That's preaching, gentlemen. The man who
in his pulpit starts with such belief in him,
with things weighted so heavily in his favour,
is almost bound to tell, to move, to win. It
is all very well for Myers to cry :

Standing afar, I summon you anigh Him,
Yea, to the multitudes I call, and say,
" This is my king: I preach, and I deny Him :
Christ, whom I crucify anew to-day."

And, indeed, we all have to fall back on that as a painfully accurate description of our case ; really yearn to lift men up to Christ, and yet keep shabbily deserting Him ourselves. " Yet this," says old John Owen, " in an especial manner is required of us who are ministers, that we be not like a hand set up in crossways directing others which way to go, but staying behind itself." This bustle of meetings, this rush of energy, this endless whirring of machinery may be all very well, but it will not do much for us. " We must go in more and more for holiness," said Mrs. Booth. Didn't Tertullian tell us that he was brought to Christ, not because he had studied the Scriptures, but because he had seen the Christians' lives, and coveted the something they possessed that resulted in that. And the faith never really spreads in any other way. When they can say of you and me what they did say of Erskine of Linlathen, that they cannot think of us and the thought

F

of God be far away, then we shall really preach to them. Remember we are meant to move among the people unconscious proofs of all we say, clear and final evidence of the enormous difference Christ makes. One flash of temper may undo more than a hundred sermons had slowly accomplished. The art of preaching! And you thought we would begin with chatter about texts and illustrations! No, gentlemen, you must start further back, if you wish real success. That then is our first basis.

And then there is this, that if you are to keep from running dry, from having only a few subjects, from boring your people by, whatever be your text, quickly jolting back into a well-worn rut, you must keep reading, reading, reading. As Quisnel put it long ago, " not to read is to tempt God, though to do nothing but read is to neglect your office."

It is true that even books are not the best inspirer of the preacher, that his own experience is far and away the deepest and the clearest of all pools from which to draw. For, so closely knit are we to one another, that even when we feel ourselves alone we are one of a seething crowd, and happenings that seem to us unique are in reality the common lot. Preach to your own heart, and many startled passers-by will stop to listen, feeling you are addressing them. Draw anonymously on the story of your life, and they will sit astonished in the pews, asking, Who has been telling him about me? Always when, as we read Father John, our heart stops short with a little gasp at the accuracy of his knowledge of us, the paragraph is sure to have the familiar ending, " this also is experience." Far separated though he was from us in circumstances, training, tradition, that vivid transcript of his soul might in essentials have been taken straight from ours. Beneath the skin, people are strangely much alike in every age, in every land.

There is a lesson for the preacher, and among the biggest of them.

No doubt a caution is required. The ways of God with souls are very varied, and we must not presume to make our mode of

things a hidebound rule for others, to claim
that because He has dealt thus and thus with
us, so it must be in every genuine case,
with every one in the true path.   There are
twelve gates into the Holy City, some facing
east, some west : and people travelling in
what appear to be diametrically opposite
directions reach the same goal.   One of the
main charms of the *Pilgrim's Progress* is
that each of the real pilgrims has had very
different experiences from the others.

Still, you remember Emerson ?   " The instinct is sure that prompts him to tell his
brother what he thinks.   He then learns
that in going down into the secrets of his own
mind, he has descended into the secrets of
all minds.   The orator distrusts at first the
fitness of his frank confessions, his want of
knowledge of the persons he addresses, until
he finds that he is the complement of his
hearers, the deeper he dives into the privatest,
secretest presentiment, to his wonder he finds
this is the most acceptable, most public, and
universally true."   And Anatole France has
the same thing in his own way :   " There is

a means of attracting which is within the reach of the most humble, and that is naturalness. One seems to be almost attractive as soon as one is absolutely true. It is because I have given myself completely that I have deserved some unknown friends. It has succeeded with me, just as it would have done with anybody else." Experience is the greatest of teachers.

Still we must keep reading and rereading. I would not like to say how often Whyte leaned over to us, with his whole soul in his face, imploring us to sell our bed, and buy this or that book. I am hopeful you may manage upon easier terms. But, even if the bed has to go, the books must be studied.

You have no idea of the enormous output in the ministry these days. Mr. Wells has been declaring that it beats him how a journalist keeps going, and still more how a minister turns up week by week with his "half hour of uplift fresh and punctual." Half hour of it, indeed! There are at least two hours as a minimum in any ordinary week. I have been calculating, and I find that, were all I preach and speak to my unfortunate people published, which heaven forbid, I should turn out no less than six large volumes of three hundred pages apiece every year ; that in my ministry so far I should have introduced into a helpless world a tiny trifle of one hundred and fifty fat and solid tomes, leaving Baxter, most voluminous of writers, at the post! There is no brain in the world that can do that kind of thing even approximately decently, without constant replenishing, especially in Scotland where we face an educated, thoughtful, able people, who are not to be put off with a snippety nothing. Sir Joshua Reynolds used to tell his students, " the mind is but a barren soil, which is soon exhausted, and will produce no crop, or only one, unless it be continually fructified and enriched with foreign matter. The greatest natural genius cannot subsist on its own stock : he who resolves never to ransack any brain but his own will soon be reduced, from mere barrenness, to the poorest of all imitations ;

he will be obliged to imitate himself, and to repeat what he has before often repeated." Even at the best you will catch yourself at that. And, within limits, it is inevitable. Is an idea to be used only once in a whole lifetime? Still, we must not let our stock become shopsoiled and worn, and dusty and befingered, but must keep adding to it constantly. See to it that in your years of preparation you lay in a huge initial store. And this the more, since what you read later does not stick in the same way.

The Testaments themselves—who can spend too much time on them, or begin to exhaust their stupendous resources? More and more, as life goes on, you will discover that labour given to them is by far the most repaying of all for the preacher; that there is no interpreter of Scripture like Scripture itself, that nothing lights it up or forms anything like so perfect an illustration for it as some apt phrase, some shade of meaning, some word or act of Jesus Christ. I would say with assurance that, if you can do that, not woodenly but freshly, then between the cleverest parallel from other

sources and a Scripture one, never hesitate
to use the latter. It will always prove the
more effective, and get deeper.

As to our formal studies it is not for me to
say anything further than this, that these
are of course simply indispensable as the
background for any decent ministry these
days, and they lead into hugely interesting
country. Only, may one straying back into
these cloistered solitudes add this, that to
confine oneself to them is apt to breed a
certain unaired mustiness in the mind, and
to cause one to lose close touch with the
realities of life. If ever you find yourself
maintaining that central doctrines are dependent on an εἰς or an ἐν, and that the
salvation of mankind totters perilously
because some MS. substitutes a ἵνα for a ὅτι,
you may be quite certain that you have lost
step with ordinary men, and that frankly
they don't believe you, are entirely sure of
this at least in a puzzling world, that that is
not the way in which a God of love would
work. And for my part, lifting up a brazen
face, I heartily agree with them. " The first

distemper of learning," says Bacon, "is when men study words and not matter."

You must of course know the great classics of the soul, you who are going to preach, must have studied with minute care God's ways with men, how He has actually drawn them, helped them, healed them. If I were on the college committee—this I know will arouse enthusiasm—I would move for yet another paper in the Exit examination, to be given five times as many marks as any other, on Practical Divinity, with questions like these :

1. Describe minutely (*a*) how Plutarch conquered his bad temper; (*b*) how Richard Baxter attained to catholicity of mind; (*c*) the remedies for shyness, that prolific source of sin, prescribed by Bunyan, Johnson, and Tennyson, stating what improvements have been suggested on their methods.

2. As illustrating the manifoldness of God's way with men, state the appeal that won Augustine, Chalmers, St.

Francis, George Herbert; giving two
other instances of each; and the differences between any one group of three.

That, of course, is a jest. For such books are
not to be studied in that fashion, but upon
one's knees. But studied they must be. It
is as scandalous for a preacher not to know
them as for a doctor to presume to practise,
never having read the ordinary textbooks.

But you must throw your net wide, must
read all kinds of things. For almost nothing to
the preacher comes amiss. Only the other
day a thing I read thirty years ago, and which
all that time had lain dustladen lumber in my
mind, rushed at a text, threw on it just the light
that I required; and, though I say it, there
was a quite admirable sermon forming itself.
" His reading," says Raleigh of Wordsworth,
" both at school and at college, was large
in amount, and was of that most profitable
kind which is called desultory."

How to retain what we read is a real
problem. Muhammad complained that, study
it as often as one might, the Koran kept

slipping away, like a camel whose leg was not tied. It is not singular in that. It is indeed pathetic what a constant loss is always leaking out. Whyte had immense faith in an interleaved Bible. I have tried that, and notebooks, and commonplace books, and most things, always with immense ardour, for about three weeks. But my untidy mind can't work like that. If yours is a more orderly one, that is the line for you. But, if it prove impossible, remember for your encouragement that neither Gibbon nor Samuel Johnson could work in that fashion any more than you. Sir William Hamilton believed in underlining, and I certainly have found it is much easier to train oneself to remember where a thing is than to carry it bodily away.

Read almost everything. Each of us must follow his own bent : but what can fail to help—art, philosophy, history, anything ? And the more you know, the more points of contact you have with other people. Denney thought that, among other things, we ought to concentrate on science, because this is a scientific age, and we must understand and speak its mental language. And certainly it is unfortunate that our theology comes from a metaphysical day, and is now in one way largely obsolete, when people are, not metaphysical, but scientific.

Biography you will find an endless mine. And in it you will be able to watch the working of these intricate minds of ours greatly more satisfyingly than in the New Psychology, which, useful though it is, is surely, may one whisper it, a little bit of an humbug, seeing that the newest of its new discoveries is well over two thousand years in age, and even then was thought a little bit old fashioned. And as Goethe says, " the most irritating of all people are clever young men who think they deny their own originality if they admit that what they think of has ever been thought of by any one before."

Frankly, I do not believe it is much use for preaching. It is true that for successful angling it is well to study the habits of the fish. But this is a mere systematizing of what every preacher, with a rudiment of common sense, does naturally and instinctively. In fact, I incline to think that to pay much attention to this matter might prove damaging to preaching. Ruskin, you remember, tells us that semi-civilized people surpass even our great artists as colourists, and explains that puzzling fact by saying that they know nothing about the laws of colour. Divert their attention to these, to the question of how it is done, and their genius for colour instantly goes out. So I imagine it might well be here. In any case it is a poor poet, as Milton says, who has to count the feet ; and a formal kind of preacher who would pause to bethink him, clutching desperately at his head, " Now to which of the three fundamental instincts should I appeal here ?"

To me the most helpful reading for preaching has been the great fiction, and, even more, letters and literary essays and the like, with their knowledge of man ; comparative religion, with its revelation of God's ceaseless quest of us ; astronomy, forcing in on the awed mind somewhat more seemly thoughts of the Majesty of God ; and above all the poets, the wonderful poets, those marvellous prophets of the Most High God. " Browning," says Hutton in one of his books, " for whom thanks be to God for ever and ever." Hearing which, my soul stands to its feet and cries with reverence, " Amen."

As to sermons, I have read hardly any for many years. That is, perhaps, one of the reasons why I cannot preach. But for most ministers, are they not a little dangerous ? Always you must be scrupulously honest in acknowledging anything you owe in any quarter, erring on the safe side in that matter, acknowledging too much and too finickally rather than too little. But is not browsing in these fields apt to make one rather like those larger ants who have small slaves to feed them ; till they have lost the power of fending for themselves, and if you take away their slaves, although in sight of plenty, they will die ? Even if you keep far away from ugly plagiarism, to transpose thought already in the shape of preaching matter wholesale to one's own mind for immediate use seems fatal. The real use of a thinker to us is that he sets

our own sluggish mind in motion, and opens up
new vistas for us to travel on our own feet.
Only if you can act like nature, can take the
leaves that fall from the stately trees, let
them sink deep into your mind, and moulder-
ing there become a rich soil out of which
something that is your very own springs up
and flowers, is it quite safe to read one's
fellow-preachers.

But further, a wise servant being asked,
" And which is Wordsworth's study," opened
a door. "This is his library," she said; " but
his study is outside." And ours must be
there too, if we are ever to be preachers.
Anatole France speaks of " bookish souls for
whom the universe is but paper and ink.
The man whose body is animated by such a
soul spends his life before his desk, without
any care for the realities whose graphic
representation he studies so obstinately. He
is monstrous and ignorant. He has never
looked out of the window." That is the
charge that is continually made against us
ministers, not, perhaps, without some truth.
At all events the world feels that we don't

know men, that we have shut ourselves into
a cramped little corner ; that we have never
looked out of the window.   And you must
look, must know the world and life, must love
your fellow-men.   For it is true, as Amiel says
of Vinet, " that it is a disadvantage to a man
to have his mind always at church."   You
remember how Lord Morley remarks of
Emerson, " He looked at life too much from
the outside ; " and then, to explain himself,
adds what he knows people will understand,
" as the clergyman is apt to do."   While
Stevenson thought that no one should be
allowed into a theological hall till he is at
least thirty.   For then we might know a little
of the world we propose to reform, and of the
men and women to whom we intend to preach.
And indeed it is true that we do start
amazingly ignorant, we who volunteer to act
as guides through life, are apt to be a little
small and old-maidish in our views, a trifle
out of drawing and perspective in our
standards, need that criticism of Johnson on
a poor soul with a finicky conscience worrying
about some sheets of paper that, in point of

fact, he had been allowed to take, " leave off tormenting your neighbours about paper and pack-thread in a world that is bursting with sin and sorrow." " Don't," said Santa Teresa, " coop your soul up in a corner." I have always regarded it as one of the most fortunate of things that I have had close friends outside the ministry, and indeed outside the church at all.

In any case life comes to our aid. For one thing, we are set down in a congregation, move about in it, and can learn immeasurably from it, especially how and what to preach. There are indeed two types of preachers. The one like Newman, a kind of mystical, mysterious figure, unseen through the week, emerging out of the Presence of God, uttering his message, and disappearing, owing something of his power to his aloofness from men. But most of us belong to the other. We must live among the people if we are to understand and help them ; must have our bookishness corrected by being brought up sharply against human wants and needs. Jonathan Edwards, indeed, alleged brazen-facedly that he just

G

could not visit. One seems to have heard
that before, and from men whose ministry,
unlike his, was not a perpetual revival.
Most ministers, indeed, seem to fret a little
over visitation as a sad waste of time. And
there are days in which we all incline to agree
with them, and have to be goaded out by
wives or other vigilant people. Still it is
essential. Whyte always said that the worst
advice he ever received was when his session
told him to preach, and not worry about
running in and out of the people's homes. For
his part, one of his devices was to adopt a
suggestion of Edwards,' and hold little district
meetings of his people here and there, delightful gatherings, where he was at his best.

Certainly it does not seem much of a hard-
ship to have the right of entrance into some
hundreds of kindly homes, where one's presence
is made welcome. Yet what to do when
there is not quite simple to determine. For
myself, I have prayer only in special cases—
illness, a boy going abroad, some joy or
trouble and the like—only then, partly for
the weak reason that to do otherwise would

quickly reduce me to a mere Buddhist praying wheel, mechanically droning out words without meaning, but partly for a weightier cause. One of the best men I ever knew told me that always before leaving a house he made a point of asking each member in turn, "Now, is there any way in which I can help you about spiritual things?" "But," I asked, "what do the young men say to that?" "It's a queer thing," he answered innocently, "that somehow since my first round they never seem to be at home"! I, indeed, feel intensely that we could do much more for our people if they would trust us as they do their doctors, and ask counsel and advice. But that somewhat crude and blunt and wholesale fashion of it will not do, is not nearly delicate enough for shy and sensitive things like souls, as fragile as a butterfly's wing, and needing as skilled handling. But to get back to our immediate point, certainly visitation is an enormous help for preaching, and will show you life, till you will know it in its deeps as few people can.

Here, for example, is one afternoon's visiting

—one day in Glasgow—not, mark you, a typical case, but, on the contrary, much the most remarkable that ever befell me ; still this thing really happened in my own experience when at my ordinary work. A doctor—a specialist— had asked me to see a patient of his who was trembling on the verge of insanity and might stumble over any hour, and knew it, telling me that medical science was helpless, that only a minister could save her. I went, and found a poor soul who had not slept for an incredible time, sitting up in bed, with furrows ploughed in her cheeks from constant weeping, imagining herself a lost soul, and fortifying her poor unbalanced mind in that waesome belief with the weirdest assortment of impossible texts gathered with a horrible cunning out of the back settlements of the Old Testament. For a full hour I wrestled for that woman's reason, feeling the powers of darkness there in the room pitted against me, at last managed to get her quieted, coaxed her to lie down and put her hands together, and say the old child's prayer ; until she fell asleep, and I tiptoed out of the room dog-tired, know-

ing a little of what our Lord must have felt
when virtue was drawn out of Him. I had
had a letter asking me to look in at a house
where the people, though not members, came to
church with us, and found that the man had
been embezzling, had been discovered, and
had fled, and there was the stunned wife
with her world tumbled in sudden ruins.
Whereat one had to comfort her, to follow
up a clue or two and find the man, to face a
furious employer, and make some arrange-
ment.   I turned into a house, to find that a
splendid young fellow, climbing rapidly to
fame in the engineering world, had that
morning touched a live wire and was paralysed
from the arms downwards, which he is unto
this day. Tired out and sick at heart, I
turned for home. But, as I was hanging
up my coat, the telephone bell rang, and an
excited voice from the far end of the city
cried to me that a member of ours had just
fallen dead, and that his wife, unnerved by
the shock, had gone hysterical and was
shrieking for the minister.   Life ! Gentlemen,
we ministers know life !

That was, of course, entirely unusual. And yet did you ever think of this, that had you passed through the villages of Palestine in Christ's time, all that you would have seen would have been the houses drowsing there in these sleepy hollows in the hot sunshine, and the children playing in the shadow, and the women singing down at the well ; would have felt how peaceful it all was, and that, could you escape out of the rush of things into this quiet, you too might make something of your soul. And yet, when Christ appeared, out from these homes there crowded all that mass of suffering, blocking the roads that led to Him, desperate to reach Him. All that had been hidden away there all the time. And visitation brings increasingly home to one what an immense weight of sorrow and anxiety there always is hidden away behind the placid faces in the pews, that always in the church there are hearts that are near the breaking, and gallant creatures making never a whimper, and yet all but spent. And it is knowledge like that that keeps a preacher to the point, that gives the right note for his sermons, that saves him from silly chatter, as Law says, about Euroclydon, and from that touch of austerity with which he is apt to begin, that adds the needed tenderness, and admiration for his fellow-men. Do you remember how a company of gipsies followed Borrow crying, " Give us God." Whereat he, fumbling in his pocket, offered them some coins. But they pitched these from them, " we don't want your money," they cried, " give us God." When a man, who knows his congregation, sits down in his study to compose a sermon, always in the silence he can hear tired voices and sore hearts and sin-sick spirits crying desperately to him, " Give us God."

How to do it ? Life will help us towards that too. The family of sorrow have a language all their own, the true accent of which no alien ever really catches. I remember twenty-five years ago meeting a young minister coming in confusion from a house of mourning. " I have never had a sorrow," he said in his honest way, " and I had nothing to say." Life with its solemn training will help

us there. As Halyburton put it on his death-
bed, " much study, much prayer, temptations
also, and distinct deliverance from temptations, are useful helps. I was fond enough
of my books, but I must say in the course of
my ministry what the Lord let me see of my
heart and what was necessary against it was
more useful to me than all my books." That
kind of thing will force us back on God. And
you remember what Denney said in criticism
of Newman's preaching, surely too harshly,
" he knew men, but he did not know God at
all." We need to know both men and God ;
and life will teach us, if we listen to it.
Gentlemen, do you realize what you are
doing when you ask to be used as a real
preacher ? Take you care : for God may
give it you, but only at the inevitable price.
Even Christ Himself, says the bold scripture,
could not have been so satisfying a Saviour,
with so delicate and sure a touch, if He had
not been made perfect through suffering.
Dare you ? Take you care : for God may hear
and answer. The art of preaching ! And you
thought we would begin with talk about

divisions and the like ! No, no, gentlemen,
you must start further back.

We have been speaking of the congregation,
and the preacher : and, between them, they
must create the atmosphere in which things
happen. For churches have each their own
climate. There are some in which a cold
waft seems to numb one, and the words freeze
and fall like snow, and melt at once into
trodden slush ; in which one has the unhappy
feeling that no one is worshipping, that the
place is more a lecture room or a concert hall
than a real church. There are others where
great swift running tides appear to seize and
lift and sweep one on his way far quicker,
surer, better than he could have gone alone.
For the Communion of Saints is a real
fact.

" You weren't in church to-day," Whyte
said to me one evening ; " where were you ? "
" I was preaching to a certain congregation,"
I replied. Whereat leaning forward he asked
eagerly, " And how did you get on ? " " I
found it very cold," I answered. " Cold,"
cried he—" cold ! I preached there two

years ago, and I have not got the chill out of
my bones yet ! "

Why is it, do you think, that evangelists
seem to secure results ; whereas, to outward
showing, our more sedate services usually
appear to lack them ? " These men are
more on fire than we are," you reply. But
that explanation does not altogether serve.
I at least can't accept it ; and for this reason,
that, when I was in my first charge, the
Simultaneous Mission was held over England,
and I was commandeered, somewhat un-
willingly, for the work. I was then young,
and could do nothing except take some of the
sermons which had been preached to my own
notably attentive people without any visible
ripple upon the surface of the waters. Yet
when delivered in these other circumstances,
every night a dozen or more claimed conversion through them. The preaching was
the same, but the atmosphere was different.
People go to these meetings expecting things
to happen. But are we not apt, both in pew
and pulpit, to put through our services as a
thing that had better be done, though, we

take it, little of course is likely to come of it ?

That is not altogether the fault of the ministry, though in part it is. " You spoke as if you had come straight from the Presence," a stranger said to Whyte. "Perhaps I did," he answered shyly. And indeed that was his settled home : and all his work was soaked in prayer. Whilst most of us are apt to overpress that claim of Hegel's, " My thinking, too, is worship."

Our fault or not, in any case it is for us to right it and make such an unexpectant mood impossible. And we can do that only if we give the people such a sense of the presence of God that they will come up to His house thrilled, hushed, eager, feeling that they are going to meet Jesus Christ—" I always do, when that man is in the pulpit, every time " —that He is certain to be there, with just that thing that their tired hearts require.

Once on a day the Battalion claimed a service right up at the front in an almost impossible place, and would take no denial. While I was arranging things, our Divisional

Commander happened to pass through the waiting groups. " A service here !" he said. " Well ! whether your padre turns up or no, I hope, gentlemen, that the Lord Christ will be with you." At which a young officer stepped forward and saluted, saying simply, " They will both be here, sir." It is when there is such an expectation that things happen, and the more that it is there, the more likely it is to justify itself. And our first duty is to waken it. Given that, the poorest stick of us will catch fire, and will really preach. And God's Spirit will be manifestly in the churches.

Ah ! gentlemen, we have a wonderful theme, and a glorious instrument, though admittedly imperfect. But the player, the poor player, with his stumbling fingers, it is he who bungles things !

In one of those irritating little studies in which,
as usual, he manages to mingle not a little
arrant wild talk, rather obviously meant to
be audacious, with much common sense,
Thoreau remarks shrewdly that many " have
an odd desire to be good, without being good
for anything." That is particularly apt
concerning preaching. We want to be good
preachers, you and I ; we would like to grip
and hold and move men, and the more the
better. But to what end, and with what
object ? Preachers, good for what ?

When by and by you will go back week by
week to your study to begin to plan out
something for the Sunday, what is going to
direct your choice of subject, and your mode
of treatment ; what is to be the aim for which
you set out, the objective toward which the
whole thing is to move, and reach it, if you
can manage it ? In this great world teeming
with interests it is not difficult, or at least it

ought not to be, to talk for five and twenty
minutes quite rationally, and sometimes even
impressively, on some subject that impinges
on life and religion. But that is not enough.
What are you out to do ? What is it that
you feel you must secure, or else your service
fails ? To be able to gather the people, to
have the church packed, it may be, that is
all very well, and seems an excellent preliminary ; but it is only a preliminary ; and
so far, from Christ's point of view, things have
not yet begun. But what happens then ?
Having got them there, what are you going
to try to do with them ? Simply to interest
them, and to get them to come back ? If
that is all, then how is Christ the better for
it ? Yes, and how are they ? It is a poor
useless business if it fizzles out in people
saying, " And I thowt a said what a owt to a
said, and I coom'd awääy " ; or, in a pleased
flutter of admiration for the preacher and
his gifts.

A sermon is a road which ought, not to die
out, but to lead to something, which those
travelling it reach. And if yours is to be a

kind of country lane, up which folk will daunder for a little while till it comes to an end, and so turn home again, precisely what they were to exactly what they left, I don't say even so it will be altogether useless. Some of them may be all the better for a breath of fresh air blown from eternity and a glimpse of the hills. Yet, surely, there ought to be some result much less vague and far more definite than that. Things should be happening somewhat as when Christ Himself appeared in a believing village : and the old signs He gave so confidently ought to be reproduced—the blind, thrilled to find a whole new world of truth and beauty suddenly rushing in upon them out of nowhere, or at least feeling their short-sightedness being corrected, and much growing clear and plain that had formerly been for them nothing but a blurred smudge, an inchoate feeling, a dim hope ; the deaf hearing quite clearly that voice of God which they had lost among the noise and jostle of life ; hearts, cold and callous to things spiritual, become warm, sensitive, tender, living ; poor creatures with unhappy, leprous lives grown clean and whole.

Anything less than that is nothing to the point. To be interesting, to grip men's minds, to hold them like a magnet, what is the use of that if it end there ? " Yes, yes," said Chalmers almost irritably when they congratulated him upon a marvellous piece of oratory in the Assembly, " but what did it do ? It had no effect. Nothing followed." To preach Sunday by Sunday, and gain nothing except his own fame seemed to him a sheer waste of time. " I am doing no good," he said, objected to the crowds, was hurt by the fact that, at his Thursday services the moment the sermon was done, the congregation drowned the prayer that followed by the rush of their departure, now the show was over. It was excitement, it was not religion, so he felt it. What is to follow your preaching if you can contrive it ? What is it to effect ? As Newman sums the matter up in the title of one of his great sermons, " The motive of the preacher is—the salvation of the hearer." Unless we are securing that, it is

sheer failure. " And remember," says Wilson,
" your salvation depends very largely on
your hearers' ! "

But salvation is a vast word. And what
for us in the pulpit, face to face with the
people, does it really mean ? What is it we
ought to be doing for them ? How are we to
bring this mighty thing and them together ?
There are many offices in the service of Christ,
and many notes in a sufficient type of
preaching. As Scripture has it, in order that
" we may all attain to maturity, and the full
measure of development which belongs to the
fulness of Christ, God grants some men to be
apostles, some to be prophets, some to be
evangelists, some to shepherd and teach."
And while the build of his mind will assign to
each of us what is to be his main function,
nowadays we have to be something of them
all ; and no preaching is adequate or rounded
that omits even one of them.

To begin with, to some ardent spirits it
comes as a shock to discover that a main part
of their lifework is to be to teach. That
daunts and discourages them. To them it

H

looks tame and unimpressive.   They want
something much more vivid and sudden and
dramatic and cataclysmic, dream of burning
words that rush folk headlong and in masses
into the kingdom.   That is possible : and we
should always keep the door wide open for it ;
and the more that we expect it, the likelier
does it tend to grow.   And yet the fact
remains that, while God does work through
the storm and fire and earthquake, oftenest
it is imperceptibly and very gradually that
His will gets itself done, and that His gracious
purposes work out.   It is a boy's dream that
war is all a glory of an huzzaing charge, with
horses at full gallop, and a broken enemy
fleeing in swift confusion.   In reality what is
needed is a dour, daily, dogged tenacity that
can hold a muddy trench for weeks on end,
with nothing visible to encourage one, content
to know that the obstinate holding on is
wearing down the enemy.

It is in that stubborn staying power most
preachers fail.   Gradually, imperceptibly, they
lose heart and expectancy, come at last to put
things through with the feeling it had better

be done, but nothing much will come of it.
Though in theory they would of course agree
that one single soul is worth the utmost pains
of the greatest minister of Christ, they begin,
in the back of their minds, to let slip their faith
in the gospel, because it is not winning the
world with quick-running machinery.

Yet, after all, no more is asked of you than
Jesus gave. What was His daily life ? To
stand immersed on a village road in a little
knot of ailing, diseased people that kept
growing as quickly as they melted away
healed : to preach at a street corner to a
group of folk, and see some of them slipping
off, not greatly impressed : to spend a long
evening with a dull old man up an alley in
Jerusalem, and a hot afternoon with a giddy
creature by a well-head. It does not look very
exciting. It did not seem to be making much
of an impression on the world. Yet it was
good enough for Jesus Christ : and He did it
day by day with a queer eagerness. And it
is big enough for you and me.

Yet some are disappointed, feel peevishly
that God is not taking them seriously, is not

making anything like adequate use of what they have to offer.

Some accept it with good humour. " You can hardly convince a man of an error in a lifetime," says Thoreau, " but must content yourself with the reflection that the progress of science is slow. If he is not convinced, his grandchildren may be." Some grow soured. Judged by its effect upon my spirit, much the most unchristian book I ever read was not even Anatole France's flippancies, when in a jeering mood, delicately destructive as the atmosphere's unseen teeth though these are, but one much praised in religious circles, " The Autobiography of Mark Rutherford." Please understand that, in spite of the quiet glory of the English, and many an apt thought, that wretched thing is a sheer libel ; that that hypochondriacal neurasthenic is no typical minister ; and still more that, though church people can be troublesome, they have no resemblance to that repulsive reptile-house of crawling, stinging, loathsome things ! Yet the horror of it is that nearly everywhere there are truths, real truths, but all misshapen as in a distorting mirror. This for example : " It was amazing to me that I could pour out myself as I did, poor although I knew that self to be, and yet make so little impression. Not one man or woman seemed any different because of anything I had said or done : and not a soul kindled at any word of mine, no matter with what earnestness it might be charged."

That is a photograph taken straight from life, a mood which every minister knows at times. Even Wesley had experience of it, on occasion. " The congregation seemed much moved," he writes one night in his Journal. " I really believe that, if they do not take great care, they may remember it—for nearly a week ! "

Yet never believe what follows, the characteristic little touch that turns truth into a leering caricature. " I did not know then how little one man can change another, and what immense and persistent efforts are necessary, efforts which seldom succeed except in childhood, to accomplish anything but the most superficial alteration of character." " Stories are told of sudden conversion," he says, but brushes that aside as a mere nursery tale.

That, gentlemen, is not only grotesque psychology, it is a sheer, deliberate, unpardonable lie. In any case, let the results be swift or slow, why should we despise this great office of teaching ? Richard Baxter was the most remarkable of preachers, with his own ministry attended by one long revival. Yet it was he who said that if parents did their duty and taught their children as they ought, preaching would soon cease to be the ordinary means of drawing souls to God.

Certainly I once had a startling experience ; sat far into the night with a minister, than whom none was more world-famous, and about two in the morning, when you will find that men silent and secretive at other times will open their minds frankly, I said to him, " Here are you, one of the most successful of preachers, here am I, a boy at the start, can you tell me how to do it ? " And he answered, " Certainly I can ! The whole art of successful preaching lies in this. Be careful to tell people only what they know already : or rather," and he put the tip of the forefinger of one hand almost at the very end of the nail of the forefinger of the other, " or rather that, and just this much more. But," added he, shifting the finger an infinitesimal bit, " if you go as far as that ahead of them you lose them to a certainty." At which I answered bluntly that, if that were so, I had no desire to preach at all. " Then I can tell you with the utmost confidence," he said, " that you will never be a popular preacher." In that spake he truly : but for the rest I cling stubbornly to my belief that his conception of things is dishonouring, though touched by a cynical knowledge of life. " Teach him to think for himself ! " cried Mrs. Shelley. "For God's sake teach him to think like other people." Not surely if we are to try to live out the great office to which we are called.

And never was teaching more required in preaching than to-day. People are confused, have doubts and difficulties, see that Christianity ought to be far more effective than it is—but how ? They need the creeds restated ; the outlook upon many central things has radically changed, and they must have them focussed anew for them. Much has been done already. And a corrective to depression, an outstanding proof of the enormous teaching power of the pulpit and the impossibilities it can accomplish, simply, slowly, imperceptibly, is the comparative ease with which the church has passed through the immense upheaval in religious thinking in our time. It has been a most remarkable achievement. And how has it been done ? How are the people learning so quickly to adjust themselves to the new outlook, in many points so absolutely novel, to see for themselves that this is not loss but sheer gain ? Primarily, of course, it is the work of our scholars, yet finally and supremely it has been due to the almost unconscious teaching of the pulpit, and that in the main not through set courses of lectures—what Lamb said of one of Wordsworth's poems is often true of them, " the instructions conveyed in it are too direct, they don't slide into the mind while one is imagining no such matters," —but simply because there has been a new atmosphere in the sermons that has told upon

the hearers, even without them realizing it.
The new climate in the pulpit has passed to
the pews.

I once saw a civilian, who had been given a
permit, being led up to his home on Frezenberg
Ridge to get some treasure he had buried. He
was told, of course, that he would never find
the place, but scoffed at the mere notion,
telling them he was born there, and knew
every foot of the whole countryside. Yet
when he reached the spot, that wild wilder-
ness with not a stone left visible, no grass,
no road, no trees, the very ridge itself half
blown away, the whole place closely pock-
marked with innumerable shell holes, he
looked a moment, turned and, weeping, went
his hopeless way. Here, too, so unfamiliar has
the landscape grown that that might well have
been the outcome on men's minds. Yet it is
not, thanks to the quiet teaching of the
pulpit. Only the other month I met a man
home from Natal, after nearly forty years,
who had just finished a tour through his native
Western Highlands. It is all changed, he
said, almost no feature of the life I knew

remains, and I passed like an alien through a strange land in the place of my birth.   And yet, he said, I would not have the old back, not one feature of it, for this newer way is far, far better !   So it is here.   Such is the pulpit's teaching power.   No doubt there is still much to do, and guiding hands are most urgently required by many who do not see their road clearly.   Quite certainly the way you will be likeliest to aid them here, too, is to let them see that you yourself know Jesus Christ, and love Him as your personal Saviour.   Once they are sure of that, once they know you are living in the Secret of the Presence, that feeling that oppresses them that the new views are a disloyalty to Christ will be swept from their minds, or at least be greatly lessened, because you believe them, and they can see for themselves that you are not disloyal, but more earnest than they are.

Even so it will need tact and courtesy and sympathy.   As Dr. W. M. Macgregor put it, speaking of the failure of one who had been somewhat rough and truculent in his shepherding of an old fashioned congregation.

" After all, no one likes to have his jaws prized open, and new truth poured down." That, I should think, is more than possible ! It is a certain half unconscious atmosphere that does it.

And then, of course, every new generation has to re-state the faith in its own mental language, to translate it into the thought of its own time, to apply it where the pinch for the moment lies. And you must do that for your own : no one else can. Things grow old-fashioned, comically so, with disconcerting swiftness. A photograph of thirty years back is a quaint affair. The clothes, the men's side whiskers, the odd shape of the women, how far away it looks from what we know ! But nothing grows so quickly out of date as sermons. There is no one, says Emerson, who would not have been entirely different from what he is if he had been born ten years earlier or later. And not one preacher in five hundred has a voice that can carry far into the next generation. Almost inevitably he is a foreigner, talking a different language from the current speech : or at least his old English sounds queer and very unfamiliar. Doctrines and modes of thought are like coins; they grow quickly blurred, dim, indecipherable, have to be called in; and new ones must be issued fresh and readable from the mint. It is *your* way of looking at Christ that will make Him visible and real to your own generation. For the herd instinct is a fact, others are dimly feeling what you feel; and you must be their mouth to state it for them, to make intelligible to them what their minds are groping after.

Still more, the deep things of God are inexhaustible: you can never come to the end of Jesus Christ: and that promise of the Holy Spirit who is to lead us further and further into all the truth is a blessed fact of life.

Peter Bell in Wordsworth's poem speaks of the villages in Yorkshire nestling in their narrow valleys, beneath the close crowding hills.

> "Where deep and low the hamlets lie,
> Beneath their little patch of sky,
> Their little lot of stars."

It is a very little patch of the broad heavens of the love of God that any one mind sees, a very little lot of stars out of that marvellous constellation we call Jesus Christ that swims into the ken of any generation. But as humanity slowly climbs the hills of time higher and higher out of the fogs and the cramped narrowness, ampler and ampler grows that all encompassing sky, more and more marvellous lights that had lain hidden rise and shine down upon their bewildered eyes. Yes, but how much there is still unseen. And every generation has to seize, and make an eternal possession of humanity, the new aspects it first finds in Jesus Christ.

Looking back, we are amazed that those behind us did not see in Him and in His teaching what to us now is so self-evidently there that it sticks out of the page. And others in turn, looking back at us, will be bewildered by the crudeness of our conceptions and our living out of Christ. Whether, as Browning held, " the first of the new beats the last of the old " or not, it ought to do so. For, as old John Duncan said, " it is we who are latest born of time, who are the real Fathers, and not the earliest Christians."

Surely, with all that training and experience behind us ! At all events, even a dwarf upon the shoulders of a giant ought to see the farther of the two. And you will have to teach, to bring home to the world those facts and implications of the inexhaustible Master that loom up to your day through the fogs of our dull, stupid, stumbling minds.

And, that apart, the Christian life common to every age, if it is a real living thing, is a continual growth and progress, a wading deeper, an understanding better, a walk with Christ, with every turning of the road opening up to us new views and glories and sufficiencies, a constant being taken aback by discovering in Him splendours for which all our crowded experiences of Him had not prepared us. Yet, to Christ's disappointment, people are apt to settle down too tragically soon, across the borders of the kingdom, but no more ; never pressing on to possess the length and breadth and fulness that is meant for them, that lies before them, theirs to take. And you, who have been set apart out of the rush of things precisely that you may be able to lead the way, are meant to be a guide helping them higher, further, deeper into the inexhaustible riches of Christ, enabling them to know Him better, building them up in the most holy faith, teaching them week by week somewhat as Christ did His disciples. It is a great office. Would we were worthier of it !

For one thing, surely, preaching ought to be more expository than it is to-day, more directly founded upon and soaked in Scripture, especially in these times when the Bible is not nearly so much read, or so well known as formerly. The passion for pretty, unexpected, out of the way texts has been much overdone. No doubt it does not take much ingenuity to make a moving thing out of " a land of far distances," or " still journeying on toward the south." All that is needed is a knack of vivid adjectives and a thrill in your voice, and there you are. Certainly the little shock of novelty may grip folk's minds. Though one questions if the mood of wondering whatever he is going to make out of that, of pleased surprise at the conjuring adroitness of a preacher who keeps producing fat rabbit after fat rabbit out of an obviously empty hat, is really that in which Christ is likeliest to reach their souls. I at least agree whole-heartedly with Denney when he says in his blunt way, " you can't in preaching produce at the same time an impression of your own cleverness, and that Christ is wonderful."

In any case it is only somewhat feeble minds that can be caught by the rather obvious trick of an *outré* text more than now and then. And it is a perverted ingenuity that wastes time hunting for them. The biggest things in life are far the most arresting. And if you want to interest people, not to say move, humble, win them, get them directly and without loss of time face to face with the cross, and the manger, and the open grave, and the wonderful figure of Jesus Christ, and the big central texts and facts. The old lecture seems gone. And courses, if you have any, must be short. But, whatever be your method, see to it that you are really expounding the faith, and not merely skirmishing cleverly on its outskirts ; that you are teaching

Christ, and not just chattering in general, in a more or less Christian way.

You remember how, in the course of his voyagings, Swift came upon Homer and Aristotle, and had the pleasant notion of introducing them to their commentators, " for they had never seen or heard of them before," due, it was whispered to the latter keeping well out of their way, " through a consciousness of shame and guilt because they had so horribly misrepresented the meaning of these authors to posterity." It was not a success. Aristotle, indeed, quite lost his temper with Scotus and Ramus ; and asked bluntly whether " the rest of the tribe were as great dunces as themselves ? " And what must Jesus Christ think of us, and the travesty that we have made too often of His glorious gospel, of our failure to see what is essential in it, of the foreign accretions that we have heaped up upon it till often it lies hidden from sight ; not least, surely, of the way we trifle in the pulpit with our time and with the wonderful Scriptures we hold in our hands. Be sure that you are keeping to the point, and preaching Christ.

I

Further, be on your guard against making a little Bible of your own, and of confining yourself to that, neglecting such parts even of the Gospels as do not so immediately appeal to your particular mind. In a sense, indeed, that is inevitable, even right. We must preach our own message, and if anything is not ours as yet, we can't really preach it. Kelman sums that up in that delightful little story in which he tells us that, feeling he was far from his great colleague's note, and ought perhaps to introduce some more of it into his own pulpit work, he tried, and was met in the vestry by Whyte saying abruptly, " Stick to your own message." Wesley, indeed, was advised to preach faith till he got it, and then because he had it. But that is dangerous counsel to my mind, that seems to lead the unwary towards an imperfect reality, and a mere throwing about of words that don't mean all that they appear to say. Still one can become lopsided in one's preaching and so misrepresent Christ; and most of the disputes in theology have arisen from people building on half-texts or on selected passages.

" Work out your own salvation." In a
rough kind of way, that is Arminianism. " It
is God that worketh in you," that is Calvinism.
But Christianity is the whole verse. Unless
you take care, you will be surprised on
examination to discover how few are the
themes you will naturally choose. Nearly
always, though not always, when a sermon
comes with a rush, your wheels are travelling
in an old rut. And we have no official Church
year to correct us. Yet it is our business to
let men see the whole of Christ ; nor can we
have Paul's ease of conscience unless, like him,
standing before a congregation he was leaving,
we too can say to ours, " Wherefore I take
you to record this day that I am pure from
the blood of all men. For I have not shunned
to declare the whole counsel of God." The
teacher has a tremendous responsibility.

At the same time a main, the main, office
of the spiritual teacher is not even to discover
to us what is new, but patiently, pertina-
ciously, obstinately, to recall to our forgetful
minds what we have learned a thousand times
and forgotten, what we have always meant

to do, yet have never actually started. As Johnson said, "It is not sufficiently considered that men more frequently require to be reminded than informed." And each time we must try to make it, trite and familiar and almost commonplace though it has grown, so vivid and impressive, that this time there will not be the usual forgetting; but the complex will be broken up, the feelings touched, the likings won, the dour will at last set in motion.

For, beyond question, what Browning calls "the real God function" is a main part of the office of the pulpit "to provide a motive and injunction for practising what we know already." And where will men find that except in Jesus Christ? That is a very deep remark of Wordsworth when he said that he preferred those of his poems that touch on the affections; for, he explained, if a work is merely didactic, it may be true yet pass. "But when a truth is linked to an affection, it is good now, and good forever." There is the secret of Christianity. It has transformed rules into a spirit, and duty into a passion, an affection, a falling in love, if one may say that reverently, with Jesus Christ. And that is what you are to bring about in those who hear you. For to teach is only one side of your task. Knowledge is not the end. And both we and our folk can easily lose ourselves in that, may talk round and round it earnestly and truly, yet never reach the vital point ; may know about Christ with accuracy, yet not know Him ; may see with clearness what we ought to do and be, yet neither do nor be it. Preaching fails if it does not induce folk to take action. We press on them the wonderful offer of God, and it is not sufficient that we get them to agree that they should take it ; they must actually do it. Here is a way of living life, Christ's way : we show it them, we urge it on them, and it is not enough that they admit that it is very beautiful and obviously what we all should be ; they must rise up and start to live it. Here is the Gospel power gifted to whosoever will accept it, and they may be moved, but unless they close with it there in the pews, and really begin to use it in their need, our effort has misfired.

Yet, for our Scottish minds there is a real danger that we rest satisfied with descriptions of the thing, that, and agreeing they are accurate. Mr. Lloyd George, you remember, told us that what struck him in reading a certain book was that up and down Scotland, at the smithies and at every street corner, they were discussing problems of theology he and his people could not follow. That is a compliment which we cannot accept as true of us to-day. For the blunt fact is that what we are discussing nowadays at the street corners and the smithies up and down Scotland is, to be honest, nothing more or less than the position of the teams on the league tables! Still there is truth in it. For good or evil, we are a nation interested in the environs of religion ; and we know it, and are apt to take that for the thing itself.

Was that what Hugh Black meant—I am the last to try to tie him down to a mere *obiter dictum* let slip in his youth—yet every hint that those who move the people drop is worth considering by us stodgier folk— was that what Hugh Black meant when he

used to say that he did not wish the people
to remember his sermon, but that his aim
was to create an emotion, a feeling, an
impression in their minds which would set
the rusty wheels of their wills turning at
last ? Robertson, of Brighton, entirely agreed.
" For myself," he said, " I would far rather
that my sermons should perish, except the
impression, the moment after delivery."

There is a great truth there, though
obviously it can be overpressed. Wordsworth
tells us that you came away from hearing Fox
with your feelings excited, and from Burke
with your mind filled. It is the latter who has
worn the better, and made much the deeper
and the more lasting impression on the world,
who has set far more wills in motion. And
a type of preaching that is all appeal would
soon wear out. But then, what Black meant
was that scaffolding is run up only that the
temple may be built within it ; and once
that is there, why, who cares any more about
the other ? Once the effect has been produced, and the step forward taken, does it
matter if the mind remembers just what it

was that pressed it into it? Our business is
is to get people to close with Christ, to
live the Christ-like life. And certainly, as
I think, in present-day preaching there is
a sad lack of this note of appeal, of urgency,
of agony, of the impression that it matters
immeasurably to them and to us that things
should come to a crisis; this eager pleading
for a definite verdict here and now. Again
and again we get people up to the point of
decision, but we don't push them over,
hardly even try. We work their minds
into thorough agreement that this and that
must be done; but we don't clinch things
on the spot. And so the metal cools again,
and nothing happens. Both Wesley and
Moody were of opinion that that is a serious
defect in Scottish preaching, that robs us of
a vast proportion of what we ought to be
reaping. It is worse than that. For there
is truth in Robertson of Brighton's grim
verdict, too sad coloured though it be. " I do
trust with all my heart that your estimate
of the effects of what you hear on your own
heart may not be delusive. I know that

spoken words impress, and that impression has its danger as well as its good. Hence I cannot even rejoice without fear, for I confess that at best, pulpit instruction seems to me to be as pernicious as it is efficacious. Still some good is done, but much less than people think. And the drawback which you correctly state is one which must always be allowed for as a large deduction from its apparent effects—I mean the absence of any immediate opportunity of carrying transient impressions into action, and the exhaustion of the feelings which are perpetually stimulated for no definite result." Surely we might greatly lessen that, if we had more skill in the definite appeal.

As things are, I am jealous for the ministry, and, while grateful, as we all must be, for many of our evangelists, feel that the ministry themselves ought to be carrying through much of their work. Do not let us exaggerate things. I, for one, claim that young communicants can be, and must be, claimed as visible results, and these likely to be more permanent than most, if they have been

properly handled ; claim, too, that there is
no necessity in every case for an upheaval
or sudden revolution in the life, that usually
the normal way of things is that one born
within the church ought to grow up naturally
in the fear of God and the definite service of
Christ. Still, more ought to be happening
than there is. No doubt the present-day
will has a keen dislike of being rushed. And
we ourselves feel uneasily that we must not
unfairly take people off their guard, so to
speak, or run them, in a moment of emotion,
into what they have not really thought out,
a feeling very markedly present in Jesus
Christ who, if He felt that some must take
the tide at once or lose it forever, would not
accept others eagerly offering, till they had,
as He said, coolly and quietly and steadily
reckoned the cost. Still the appeal, the call
for a decision now, the pressing for a verdict,
ought to be a feature in our preaching.

And how are we likeliest to gain a response
to it ? What, in our day, are the notes that
thrill to actual action ? Some, once much
used, are laid aside, or nearly so. Perhaps

too much. Every one tells us, for instance, that fear never kept any one from any sin. I am not sure of that. Fear was a very real appeal at one stage of human history; and one must remember that no human type dies out, that in our modern world there are still very primitive people. In any case, fear is not always cowardice, it is sometimes an awed and honest facing of tremendous facts. When science corroborates the faith, as it does so eloquently, telling us that this is certainly a moral world, governed by laws which are not merely good advice, but laws with grim sanctions attached, and that inevitably what a man sows he must reap, the feeling that breeds in the mind can be called fear, yet it is wholesome, and does keep from sin, partly by shattering ignorance. And in our day that is undoubtedly an effective, though not perhaps the loftiest, appeal.

Probably the most successful of all for the moment is the call to service. That is largely what lies behind this talk about a " social gospel," to me an unfortunate phrase. Since, in the last resort, no problem, social or any other, will ever be solved except by the creation of new individuals. And one fears that to-day folk are forgetting that, even in pulpits sometimes, are giving many the impression that some change, external to themselves, can in itself work the miracle of the new earth wherein righteousness will dwell, without them bothering to lose their grub-like ways or to grow wings and become new creatures. But the sunny side of it is that the new generation appears to be much attracted by the Master's teaching of a kingdom that claims them and their service, that is out to win the world, to touch and transform every department of man's life with the glory of Christ, and summons them to play their part to this great end. It is not what Christ gives, but what He asks, that moves them. And that begets a very winsome, practical, and effective, if a somewhat shallow, type of Christianity. It is what youth is offering Christ to-day.

But you remember how, when Christian was asked what it was that sometimes gave him a lift forward on his way, he replied,

" When I think what I saw at the Cross,
that will do it ; and when I look upon my
broidered coat, that will do it ; and when I
look into my roll, that will do it ; and when
my thoughts wax warm about whither I am
going, that will do it." So, were I asked
what in my own little experience I have found
brings people to the point, I should answer,
first, what I often saw at the front. I should
not like to say how many boys just out for
the first time came to me and said nervously,
" Padre, I am uneasy. Not that I am afraid
or have any reason to doubt myself. But
I have had a sheltered life, and have never
been tried or tested. Now that I am up
against it, how do you think that I shall do ?"
And always I replied, with confidence, "you are
going to do splendidly ; and I shall tell you
why. You are now wearing the uniform of
a superb battalion ; and everybody in it
will assume, as a matter of course, that you
are going to be worthy of it. And you will
discover that that trust in you will help,
almost compel, you to justify it ; that that
quiet assumption will make it nearly im-

possible for you to fail." And again and again
they came later, saying that they too had
found it so. There, surely, is more than a
hint for us preachers. "If," said Goethe, "you
want a man to be big, assume that he is big,"
and every one cries out at his genius. But
is that not the very foundation of the teaching
and method of Christ ? That quiet assumption in our preaching that men born in the
church are of course going to be true, and that
for them it is nearly impossible, surely, to fail,
helps more, as I believe, than the fiercest
denunciations, or the most glowing appeals.
" That will do it."

And then there is the Cross. It was not for
nothing that Christ said so confidently that
always if men see Him dying for them, He
will win. Certainly it has not always been
at Calvary that their hearts have been most
moved. It makes an interesting study to
note how different generations have been
won mainly by different things in Christ.
And to-day we seem back at the outlook of
sub-apostolic times, in this respect at least,
that the young generation seem to be most

drawn to the Wonderful Figure going about
doing good. And yet in every age there are
always those who cannot come within sight
of the Cross without being thrilled and moved
and won, for whom that is the deepest and
the most appealing of all facts. And nobody,
surely, can remain face to face with it quite
untouched. Get them in sight of Calvary,
pause there, saying little, hushed and reverent;
enable them to look, to see it, make it real to
them, not just an old tale that has lost its
wonder and its stab, but a tremendous awful
fact. That still constrains men, that " will
do it," that will almost always do it, for the
older people of our day who have themselves
given their sons, and watched and waited
in an agony perhaps of years, and bowed
their heads with proud submissiveness at
last. For them the chief appeal that almost
cannot fail to win them is the huge self-
sacrifice of God, the blessed and amazing
fact that He too gave His Son. Yes, that
will almost always do it for those whose own
hearts so understand. There, then, is the
metaphor which best explains Calvary for

our generation. Speak of it in terms of
sacrifice, as the writer to the Hebrews does,
and we, who know so little of the sacrificial
system, do not follow easily. State it as
Paul does in his more metaphysical moods,
and we limp somewhat lamely after him.
Many of the explanations given by church
Fathers do not help, they hinder us. But
preach it in terms of God's self-sacrifice, as a
tremendous revelation of the life He leads, of
how He is hurt by the sins and sorrows of the
world, and how He spends Himself un-
grudgingly on our behalf who merit nothing
but His anger, with no thought but to heal
and help and save, whatever be the cost of
that to Him, and our minds follow, and our
hearts are won. But however you may put
it, preaching must have that note of appeal
in it somehow.

When Boston was a probationer, a lad of
22, he wrote a soliloquy on the "Art of Man
Fishing," a gathering together for his own
eyes alone of some thoughts upon how to
preach. The most skilful angler, who can
cast far and sure without a ripple on the

waters, and who knows every fly for every pool, will not make much of things if there is never a hook. And let your art be what it may, if you have no appeal, you, too, are like to trudge home in the evening with an empty basket.

But yet again, when you sit in your study thinking of the coming Sunday, you must remember this, that most of those to whom you are going to speak will be Christian people, very many of them finding it a hard and difficult fight. They will be tired, some of them disappointed, all of them tempted, not a few discouraged and at their wits' end. The mass of trouble in a congregation is quite unbelievable. And they come up to church, looking to you to help them, hoping for some word that will bring them through. Remembrance of that will often fix your choice of subject, and your mode of treating it.

Once as a lad I was present at a gathering of distinguished ministers, when the question was raised, " What ought to be the main note in one's preaching ? " Various answers

K

were suggested, no two being the same, till
Principal Martin, then in his charge, won
them to unanimity by saying that the older
that he grew, the more he felt that the stress
should be laid on " Comfort ye, comfort ye
my people, saith your God." I am older
now than he was then, and the years have
been steadily teaching me too that same
lesson. Remember they are tried, some of
them near the breaking-point, and comfort
them. Wesley speaks several times in his
Journal, with unusual heat, of the fact that
here and there he came on congregations
who had stopped trying. And usually, he
maintains, the reason is that they have had
far too discouraging preaching, some of it
quite unduly severe, and nearly all of it not
merely holding up a huge ideal for them (that
we must do, for God will not be satisfied
until we are like Christ), but stunning them
into a feeling that for them at least it
evidently is no use to try at all. That is just
wicked.

Surely the main notes that ought to
characterise a Christian service are a wonder-

ing happiness at finding that God has not turned from us, but still forgives us, still believes in us, is somehow still entirely sure that we can, even yet, do well ; and a new rush of hope, finding that He has not lost hope for us, kindling our own spent light at His, which all the gusts have not blown out ; and a glorious renewal of our sense of God, a feeling that our "dowieness" was silly, could have been due only to our having forgotten that He was there beside us ; whereas, now we have remembered it again, see it again, what need we fear ? For God and we together, can we not manage to face anything? Unless they find themselves in God's very presence, unless they feel His healing touch on them, unless they pull themselves together, sure that they can do it—and they shall—our sermon fails.

Yes, but what God ? None but the God we see in Jesus Christ will meet men's case. Whatever else we do, they must come upon Him ! And we must start determined upon this, that, please God, we are going to bring Christ in among them, to carry them in their helplessness to Him, like the sick in a village through which He was passing, to set them and Him together face to face. That is our job, and we must try to do it. For nothing else will serve.

Often out at the front I used to ask the men, " What shall I preach about ? " And they never asked for anything about the war, or intellectual difficulties. Frequently they said nothing at all. But not seldom a man would say " Tell us something about Jesus Christ." That is what they needed yonder, face to face with death. And that is what they need here, face to face with life, which, says Paul, is a far deadlier enemy.

An egregious idiot of a confident critic from the other side of the Atlantic has been moving about the country, declaring that none of our ministers know how to preach at all. " Bless me," he cried, " they can speak of nothing except Jesus Christ."

I thank God for that criticism, hostile though it was meant to be. Nothing so interests, nothing so helps, nothing so rallies as a glimpse of the Saviour. And you are here to give it to your people.

Only once was a sermon of mine completely successful, and that only to one hearer. It was preached in a little village ; and, during its delivery, I noticed in the front seat a distinguished looking man, obviously an American, with a curiously rapt look on his face. But it was months afterwards I learned —it was Hubert Simpson who told me—that that worshipper had had a strange experience. When the sermon began, somehow he saw Christ standing behind the preacher ; and, as it proceeded, the latter faded out, and for him there was no one there except our Lord, and he was looking straight at Him. Thousands of times though I have preached, no other human being, so far as I know, ever experienced anything the least like that. Yet, if we knew our business, and did it thoroughly, that is what ought to happen every time. Remember, as you fasten on your subject for the Sunday, that the people hope that you are coming from the Secret of the Presence with a message in which they will catch that urgent and imperative " Thus saith the Lord," and feel something of the Master's tenderness ; that you are going to stand in Christ's place, and to speak Christ's word, and to act as Christ's representative. Ah ! no doubt He is He, and we are only we, and between Him and us there is a great gulf fixed. And yet, says Paul, it is on Christ's behalf we come ; it is in Christ's stead we beseech you ; it is as if God Himself were pleading through our lips we speak this we have brought from Him to you.

What would Christ say to them ? That is what we must try to say.

SUPPOSE yourselves, gentlemen, settled in a charge, that a Sunday is over, and your Monday round of golf put in. For let me impress upon you with all earnestness, that whatever your form of it may be—and you remember Samuel Johnson's complacent boast that though too short-sighted for games, he had managed to idle wonderfully well without them—some regular exercise is for most men a first essential of true preaching, a necessary preventive of those black fumes and humours that otherwise are apt to gather in the mind, vastly increasing the difficulty of our work, and greatly lessening the worth of it.

I know a man who asserts that far and away the best lesson on preaching he ever received was given him by a pawky country doctor, himself a close friend of God, who, if the sermons had been gloomy on the Sunday would drop in, and remark enquiringly, " A

little liverish weren't you, yesterday ? I
thought I would look in and recommend
some exercise." Every one nowadays knows
how closely interlaced are body and spirit ;
but nowhere is Browning's somewhat exaggerated view " nor soul helps body more, than
body soul " so near literal accuracy as in
preaching. If your brain seems choked,
clogged and sticky and out of gear, there is
no need to fall back on desperate explanations
such as that God has forsaken you. Better
begin, at least, by much humbler enquiries ;
and this among the first. " Have I been taking
reasonable care of the tools which God has
given me with which to work ? " It is
unfair, it is a wrong to Jesus Christ, not to
speak of the people, to stand glooming in the
pulpit simply because, unconsciously, we
have let ourselves get a bit out of sorts, and
life looks grey to us. The pathological and
climatic background of the great spiritual
classics would make an interesting study.

I wouldn't wonder if the bracing atmosphere
of Aberdeen added a little to the sheen and
glow of Rutherford's Letters. At all events

it is to those that he wrote there that I keep turning. And could Boston have been so spiritually nervous and hypochondriacally self-centred in that glorious home of his nestling yonder among the green Ettrick hills, if he had not shut himself up so straitly in his stuffy little study ? At all events some of the deepest of the Roman Catholic masters upon prayer lay urgent stress on this, that it is so tiring a business that one has no right to look for marked success in it unless one is prepared to take all pains to keep the body as fit as one can. And that is no less true of preaching. Fail there, and when you reach the pulpit your voice will lack resonance, or your spirit be lethargic, or your mind be dull and sluggish, or your outlook on the world be dimmed. The lilt, the lift, the glow that there should be in preaching, may be absent.

Suppose, I say, that it is Tuesday morning, and another Sunday is looming up, rushing in on you suddenly like a steamer in a fog, there before you know. The first business is to fasten on your subjects. As a rule there

is small difficulty—I can give you that encouragement—in lighting upon texts. For
this is an interesting world, and Christ is
an inexhaustible subject. Often, indeed,
you will be bothered by a plethora of
claimants clamouring for attention, and
may lose time deciding between them. One
cannot, as a rule, take up the Bible, but
things leap out of the flatness of the page
and clutch at us demanding to be preached
upon. A light falls, sudden and almost blind-
ingly, on what we had never seen before, often
though we have read it, and there is a great
truth staring up at us. I cannot tell how
often, reading the Scriptures at a service,
texts for the next week have run out at me,
disturbingly enough, and have had to be
pushed roughly aside. Or, if you have learned
how to use your books, and that takes time,
unless you are very fagged, your ordinary
reading will send ideas tumbling over one
another into the mind. A sentence here
will give you a sermon ; a phrase there opens a
vista new to you. Often the whole thing is
built up round a quotation that occurs in it,

not a dozen words in length ; that was the starting-point, what set your mind in motion. Frequently something that grips you leaps at a kindred or at an opposing text, and there is your sermon forming itself. When, to take any random instances, you come on Morley's gloomy finding, after his immense experience of life, that for the wettest of wet blankets give him the man who was most of a visionary in his youth, and with that there rises up before you Paul's brave saying, " and experience worketh hope," there evidently is your line, one thing that grows bigger and better in a disillusionizing world. Or when Dostoieffsky tells us that he wishes he were an insect to escape the pangs of humanity, and at that there comes the thought of Calvary with its solemn revelation of God's life as a huge, endless self sacrifice, the question asks itself, and upon which plan am I living mine, insect or God ? Or when Goethe, you remember, almost parodying that saying of Christ in which He sums up His constant sense of the immeasurable prodigal lavishness of God from which no unworthiness on our part can sour Him, bids us be unlike Nature, who, says Goethe, has no feeling, for does not the sun shine on the evil as well as the good, and are not moon and stars for the unjust as well as for right-living folk—the same fact that so struck Christ, but how differently interpreted, making Goethe bitter—there surely is a striking instance of Christ's characteristic way of taking things by the golden handle, as Epictetus used to say, with endless applications—Man, life, the Cross, God's ordering of our days bursting in every-where. Why take the gloomy view, seeing there is another, very blessed one, as likely, aye, far more. Believe me, as a rule there is no dearth of subjects.

But there do come dreadful times, with some frequency in the early years, though growing, let us own it gratefully, increasingly seldom, when the mind seems a sheer echoing blankness, and the Bible itself empty and sapless, and nothing that one reads has any taste in it, or any suggestiveness whatever, dull, ugly days in which, as Dods used to say, you will wish ardently that you were a stone-breaker, anything indeed except your own impossible job.

Sometimes that experience means that one is tired ; often it is a kindly danger-signal hung out in warning ; not seldom, I believe, it is part of our moral discipline. For I have noted that if ever I am just a little bit puffed up, have a pleasant feeling that a service was not bad for me, one of these barren times is apt to fall suddenly out of a clear sky. And certainly they are amazingly effective in making one realize that he is a poor useless creature, utterly dependent upon God.

None the less, obviously we ought in times of plenty to lay up for such lean days, which, believe me, come to every one. If ideas for sermons strike you, if texts offer themselves in groups, be sensible, and write them down in a book, always with some suggestion of the line you mean to follow. For, otherwise, you may later stare stupidly at them, the thought flown, with not an idea what you were to make of this. To be honest, the book has nearly always beaten me, stupidly enough. If that be so with you, have recourse to the backs of envelopes or anything, though you are often likely to be irritated by blurred jottings become indecipherable, possibilities that have vanished into thin air, leaving just enough to make you feel how good they would have been! Without a doubt a book is the real thing. Sometimes you will have to put down a text, feeling there is a sermon in it, but not seeing it as yet. An old friend of mine always had a notion that some day he was going to write a great sermon upon " linen clean and white, which is the righteousness of saints," yet he died without ever coming upon what he felt was there, though curiously enough the moment he spoke of it to me a sermon leapt full-grown into my mind. Think of the weaver's shuttle, clicking to and fro, and slowly, one thin thread by one thin thread, building up the web, so is it that the glory of the redeemed saints is won, one little duty added to another little duty, till there is all that sheen and glistening of splendour.

But if ever your book runs dry, and a bad time comes, remember above all things, first, to consume your own smoke in the study, and not carry a miasma of wretchedness through the whole house; and, second, that you must keep cool, though precious time is running past with nothing done, must not get fidgety and nervous, scurrying wildly here and there through the fluttering pages of the Bible, but must fasten doggedly upon a subject and stick to it resolutely. That is a first law. Otherwise this chopping and changing may become a weekly habit, with miserable consequences to your peace of mind. One of the greatest preachers in the land was for many years a martyr to that kind of thing; would start, and fling it down, and try another passage, and go back to the first, and sicken of them both, and so on endlessly, till Saturday evening sometimes found him still without a text, and by this time in a nervous fever. Until necessity compelled him to choose something, and he would sit up all Saturday night and write a superb sermon, as he would have done at any time during the week on almost any of the subjects, had he only stuck to it, and with how much less mental strain and cost and agony to himself. Even the great Candlish of Disruption days suffered terribly from this disease. Having got your subject, start on it at once, always, if possible, early in the week. On Tuesday, let us say, draw out a rough outline of the road you mean to take, and not only work at it in your forenoons in the study, but as you go about your visiting and other tasks, let your mind keep travelling back to it from time to time, and take another turn of teasing at it, and shaking it about like hay ; and so away again, and by and by back once more. For I wish to say a thing that some of you may easily enough misunderstand and misapply. That cannot be helped. If, says the Scripture bluntly, you have a vision, tell it. The wise man will be the better of it, and as for the fool—well, he is a fool in any case ! If any person is so far left to himself as to imagine that anything I say can be twisted to mean that one can loaf into skill in preaching, he is dreaming the vainest of dreams. As Reynolds told his students, " The impetuosity of youth is disgusted at the slow approaches of a regular siege, and desires from mere impatience of labour to take the citadel by storm. They wish to find some shorter path to excellence; and hope to obtain the reward of eminence by other means than those which the indispensable rules of art have prescribed. They must therefore be told, again and again, that labour is the only price of solid fame, and that, whatever their force of genius may be, there is no easy method of becoming a good painter." Or, as Voltaire has it, "Difficulty is the tenth muse." Genius, thought both George Eliot and Carlyle, and Newton said it before them, consists of an immense capacity for taking pains. I am not certain about that; but the chances are enormous that you will never preach well unless you work desperately hard at it. Only there is this to add. At first when things were moving heavily, I used to sit doggedly at my task, toiling laboriously for long hours with little to show for them. And that was a fine moral discipline. But it was not the way, for me at least, to get the sermon finished, and that in the best form.

L

One stuck at it so long that one lost taste for it, grew sick of it, preached it at last with little interest in it oneself. For me, when these times come, it pays far better to work hard and, if things stick, after an honest effort to turn to something else, and so back to the sermon later, often with the happy result that the subconscious mind has been at work upon it, and things have cleared in a surprising fashion, and one gets under way with a fresh breeze blowing cheerily behind one, saved from ennui and the doldrums and fidgetiness and worse—still eager on the subject. So at least, I have found. But, to be safe, one must start early in the week.

It is true that the mind works quicker and quicker as a rule as one gets expert at one's work; and especially you will find that often after a rushed week, it answers to the spur in a surprising fashion. " All enduring literary work," says Sir Walter Raleigh, " is the offspring of intense excitement." There indeed, lies a danger. For you will learn that often it is the sermons that were dashed off, either because they formed rapidly in the

mind, or because one was cramped for time
towards the week-end and had to hurry them,
for which one is thanked. There is in that a
temptation indeed, but also a useful hint
worth our remembering—this, namely, that
while we sit looking at the thing for a long
while in the study, thinking it over and over,
the hearers only have it spoken to them once,
and we can easily heap in too much to make
it really effective as heard, though we may be
improving it as written, and could it be read.
Still, better have too much stuff than too
little. I have heard Parker preach sermons
awesome for their fulness and impressiveness.
Yet once the thing was nothing short of a
colossal fiasco, and that from sheer tenuity
and lack of matter! He took as his subject
how Jacob made off with Laban's idols. And
the whole thing was nothing more than a
dramatic retelling of the story. He tip-toed
about the pulpit, furtively he concealed the
hymn book, we saw the flight and the pursuit,
and were told of the lassie sitting on the
idols. There was not an attempt at expounding or applying till the last sentence

when he suddenly drew himself up, and using the full compass of his mighty voice, shouted, " My friends, believe me, a god that can be sat upon is not the true God." And that was all, from a mind teeming with ideas ! And I, standing in the aisle, could hear again that fellow-countryman of mine, when James I of England asked him what he thought of his favourite court-preacher, Bishop Andrewes, answering bluntly, " It is not preaching, it is playing with his subject." Put stuff into your sermons. Yet we can put too much !

Do not allow yourself delay beginning till late in the week, for that makes for an unhealthy life and feverish work. I know a man who erred the other way, who had his forenoon sermon largely written before he went to bed the previous Sunday night ; and this because he found that his brain worked so quickly then. That I can well believe ; but also, what he came to find, that the copy that it then threw off was apt to be excitable and turgid, and that in any case he was encroaching on his capital of nerves and strength. Tuesday forenoon is soon enough, though Whyte was always at his desk by 9 o'clock on Monday morning.

In your choice of subjects, bear some things in mind. And this first, that you are always going to treat the Bible honestly and reverently. Let me illustrate what I mean. One of the greatest preachers in our land once insisted with some excitement that I should go with him (we were both on holiday), to hear what he declared was the most satisfying preaching he had heard for a long while. And in truth the officiating minister was a man with a huge reputation. We went, and took part in a service notably beautiful and helpful. But, when the sermon came, my mind rose in revolt and passionate protest. It was on the three raisings from the dead, and the idea was that our Lord worked the miracles, not out of compassion for the mourners or the like, but because He needed—so we were told—" a peg " on which to hang some part of His teaching; and here it was, God-given. When, for example, He raised the widow of Nain's son, the reason for the act lies in the words, " and He gave him back to his mother." Christ, it seemed, wished a chance of teaching us that in the other world we shall receive and know our own again ! My friend stood to it dourly that it was great preaching, and that he himself was much impressed. To me it seemed dishonest, and something approaching blasphemy. You have no right to twist the word of God into any shape you choose, or to make anything out of it that comes into your mind. Be reverent and honest towards the Bible.

Further, here is another little anecdote leading up to another rule. When I was still at New College, Whyte asked me to preach in St. George's ; and the time being far ahead, and being flattered, I consented, though when the thing drew near I struggled desperately to escape, in vain. It was a very wretched youth that crept into the pulpit, and his discomfiture was made complete by seeing Rainy in the congregation. That great soul walked home part of the way with me, and, among other things, said this: " You chose a great subject. That was right. You cannot always do it. But do it as often as you can." That, I believe, was very sound advice, though it is not the easy path. So long as we are pirouetting with some pretty bit of a text on the outskirts of things, we feel fairly easy in our minds. But it is a very humbled creature who stands up to preach on some tremendous central passage such as " God so loved the world." Well, to begin with, we are likelier, I take it, to be used in that mood than when we are feeling fairly cocksure. Moreover, the glorious passage may linger about the people's minds, though they reject our sermon on it as pathetically inadequate. In any case it is well sometimes to throw oneself in bodily into such unfathomable things as the opening passage in Ephesians, or the end of the eighth of Romans, or the story of the Prodigal, or the wonderful words in the Upper Room, to feel our feet plucked from beneath us by tremendous tides, and vast and towering billows crashing over us, sweeping us helplessly far out into infinite deeps. It is part of your duty to bring home to people that this faith of ours is not a pond round which you can stroll in half an hour, and at the end say, " There it is, you see," but a tremendous shoreless sea ; that there are awe on awe, and mystery on mystery, and marvel upon staggering marvel heaped up in it. What does it matter about our poor little reputation if through our very stammering failure they see something of the bigness of Christ, and the amazement of God's love. Even the Apostles tell us they feel they are failing, that their stuttering gives no adequate idea of Christ. Even Luther said that the best preacher, face to face with Him, is but a baby gooing and gurgling, using half words and quarter words.

Still, we are here to preach the person and faith of our blessed Lord and Master ; and we dare not avoid the deepest and most central features of that, because of our incompetence to do them justice. Maclaren of Manchester is worthy of all honour for the lead he gives us in this vitally important matter.

Further, do not be abstract in your sermons. Theological you will have to be, but let it not be of the formal kind. Preach, not doctrines,

but Christ. Let them see that Wonderful
Figure : and, as you talk of Him, they will
all grasp what you think about Him, and, if
you are successful, will agree with you.
Whereas, if you preach doctrinally, in the
sense of handing out cold slabs of abstract
theorizing, they will cease to listen, or get
lost. Wesley in one place tells us that he
preached in a certain church, " but not upon
justification by faith," adding that he " did
not find that a profitable subject for an
unawakened congregation." No ; that is not
the way to lure men to Christ. Show them
the Saviour in action ; let them see Him
dealing with Zacchæus or with Mary Mag-
dalene. That will do it.

Courses are not in fashion, as they once
were. And yet some courses you are almost
bound to have ; one for the class at least, and
probably another for the Week-Night Service.
For that last, remember, you must prepare
carefully. For then you are likely to be shut
in with some of the most spiritually-minded
of the people, both can and ought to get " far
ben." Our Lord spoke wonderful words to

anyone who would listen, but his deepest
when He was alone with His friends. And
we too, not perhaps just at the very start,
but by and by, ought to feel that we have
most to say that matters, can get nearest
God, can open our hearts the fullest and the
best, when we are in a circle of those who live
very near Him.

The same thing holds about wet Sunday
evenings. At first, if you are normal, they
will awaken in you a vexed feeling that your
labour has been largely thrown away. And
that, perhaps, never entirely passes. But
more and more as time goes on, when you
face a small company on a wild night, your
heart will run out to those who are there with
a more than usually keen desire to reward
them and to give them something that will
really help them. But to come back to
courses ; as to Sunday services, you will, I
think, find it to your own advantage to preach
through the central matters about Jesus
Christ and the culture of the spiritual life
in a series of courses, fairly short. These can
be very varied. Whyte, indeed, gave out the

same text each forenoon for, I think, four years,
" Lord, teach us to pray." But from that
basis he swept his congregation through the
whole difficult art of prayer, and then the
Prayers of the Old Testament, and those of
Christ, and those of Paul, a marvellous
experience, with him as guide. Yet, even so,
some of the congregation found it tending a
little, perhaps, towards monotony. Courses
should certainly be short and varied. And
there is no doubt that, upon the whole, people
to-day prefer the interest and novelty of
isolated texts.

One type of subject you will find, if you
have any skill at it, and use it only occasion-
ally, never fails to grip—a study of some
character. Dr. Sclater indeed differs, and
he ought to know. One heard many eager
testimonies to the helpfulness of his course
under this foundation, as was only natural,
for who has a better right to speak
about preaching ? But one discouraged man
reported, I suppose with some exaggeration,
that the lecturer had, half in jest I take it,
belittled this as the last refuge in a storm.

And that had daunted him, for any fruits he had had in his ministry had come from sermons upon characters. And I can well believe it. With all diffidence, though I agree so far with Dr. Sclater as to use this method myself very seldom, it simply will not do to push aside as a poor kind of makeshift thing a type of preaching of which many of the mightiest masters have been obviously fond, and into which they heaped their best, and through which they produced their most electric effects. Read, for example, A. B. Davidson's "Called of God," and you will see with a wondering envy, what can be done through preaching of this type. It requires, indeed, certain gifts, especially the power of thinking oneself into another's place, and looking through his eyes; some of that uncanny faculty that Browning shows so perfectly in "The Ring and The Book"; but, given that, you are sure to succeed. If you are unimaginative, let it alone. But if you can lose yourself in the other, then, because under the surface differences these hearts of ours are much alike, Pilate or Zacchæus will speak to your people with a queer haunting power, and God's word become strangely vivid to them.

Having got your subject, you must break it down, arrange it, build it up. And that brings us to heads, on which matter I am a heretic. A very distinguished scholar once said to me with almost truculent confidence, as if stating an obvious fact, that there never had been a notable preacher who did not use them, and was much astonished when on the spot I was able to rattle out some of the greatest who never employed one in their lives. And, indeed, it is a mere pulpit illusion that by the natural law of things all truth, like all Gaul, falls into three parts. It is very handy when it does, as in a verse like " that ye may know what is the hope of His calling, and what the riches of the glory of His inheritance in the saints, and what the exceeding greatness of His power to usward who believe," where your sermon is offered you as a gift, and its type fixed. But then there are sermons and sermons. One kind, and in a master's hands it is among the most effective, has really only

the one dominant idea, speeding straight to its
goal as swiftly as an arrow's flight.   In it you
want no heads.   Hence Newman denounced
heads, declaring it just means three sermons.
Another (Roman Catholic preachers often
use it) takes a central theme and muses on it,
turning it round and round, and always at the
end of every section presses it home upon
you ; heads if you like, but really rather
differing facets of one thing.   Another, which
to me when in the pew proves about the
most arresting and helpful of all, is like a full
mind unrolling itself, throwing in heaps of
things, but always moving on to a definite
goal, leading you following eagerly far further
and far deeper than you know, till the end
comes with you holding your breath, because
God is so very near—a kind of Boswell of a
sermon that at first sight seems to have no very
definite plan, yet is really consummate art,
more so even than the neat pieces of carpentry
with their sweet-smelling wood and delight-
fully smooth edges.   But that is much the
hardest type, and requires far the greatest
experience and skill.   As a rule, we need

heads. But, in my judgment, they ought to be kept as much as possible out of sight. A painter has to study anatomy, or his figures will be wobbly and misshapen. But he does not let you see the backbones sticking through ! And to announce one, two, three, seems to me very crude, and desperately poor psychology. There is no need to invite the attitude of mind of a bored traveller, whose book is stale, and the papers dull, and who, hearing " secondly," looks moodily out of the window, and mutters " only Newcastle, and hours and hours still till we get to Inverness." Always when a man thrusts his heads into prominence, he has on announcing each of them to gain my attention all over again; whereas if he had not jolted me when he ran across the points, he would have held me to the end. Still, usually one must have heads in one's own mind, at least, if we are to preserve balance and due proportion. And one can easily enough fail there. Taylor Innes was reputed to be in his day the best judge of preaching in Scotland, and he used to say to me that one ought to begin fairly far out on the circumfer-

ence and work one's way in to a centre, ever
rising in passion and earnestness and entreaty.
Perhaps ; but nowadays in this hurrying age
it is often well not to lose much time on an
introduction, but to take a header into the
main thing you want to say. At all events,
you must have balance and proportion, must
not spend the whole time in running up to
the wicket, and have none left to bowl the
ball and get your man out ! I once heard
Fairbairn of Mansfield, who had often stunned
my wondering mind by the brilliance of his
antithetical preaching, dazzling as a blinding
flash of sword-play almost too fast to follow,
preach for fifty minutes, and end by announcing that this was his introduction, and he
had not come in sight either of his sermon or
his text. Something had gone wrong somewhere ! And, if you are to have set heads,
choose them skilfully, studying such a master
in the art as Watkinson. Once in the
Western Highlands I heard a man, a good
soul who knew what he was speaking about,
but had not attained much art in preaching,
after some minutes announce that he was to

prove his case, "first, by the whole word of God, second, by all human history, and third, by the whole of your experience." Starting with Adam, he got as far as Moses under head one, and then lost heart at the enormous tracts before him. "And, and, and all the rest of them," he said, and hurried to head two, but had scarcely begun, when the Gaelic people, waiting for their service now long overdue, burst in indignantly, and the thing fizzled out without head three at all. Still, heads well chosen and, in my view, left unobtrusive, are extremely valuable. For, as Erskine of Linlathen said after a long sombre silence coming home from listening to a vague loose kind of omnium gatherum of things in general, " the educated mind desiderates a nexus."

Having got your ideas arranged so far in order, your next point is, are you going to read or speak your sermon ? For, although much I shall now say may seem to tell precisely the other way, that really goes a long road to determine how your sermon is to shape itself and be built up. For, as John Caird that great

M

authority tells us, the arts of writing and of
speaking are so vastly different that the very
excellencies of the one may easily become
sheer flaws and actual hindrances in the other.
That I believe is where our ministry often goes
wrong, and loses much of its effectiveness.
Our minds are trained to write, and not to
speak.   And even when we do speak, we are
still speaking in the writer's way.   Yet
everybody knows that most of the speeches
that swept the crowd who heard them make
commonplace reading ;   and on the other
hand that Burke, whose least written word
will live as long as the English language, was
almost entirely ineffective when upon his
feet, so much so that there were cases of great
judges holding as not worth an answer
speeches which, when they read them, left
them stunned.   So was John Morley.   Listening to him, one was greatly disappointed ;
but read it next day, and how masterly it was.
There have been exceptions ; Lord Rosebery,
for instance, spoke in the writer's way and
amazingly tellingly.   Yet, on the whole, a
spoken and a written thing ought really to

be built up very differently. And yet I am going to say what seems to fly right in the face of that. There are three possible methods in the pulpit : reading, speaking, and more or less memorizing what one has written. The last never has a good word said for it. Always it is denounced and ridiculed, in a way that is simply ignorant and silly—looking to the long array of great orators in politics and in the church who either used it to the end, or more commonly as a half-way house to something vastly better. One of the three or four most effective speakers in politics to-day, for example, has written a long article in which he frankly confesses that the large basis of all his brilliant speeches, little though anybody would believe it, so natural, spontaneous, coruscating is it all, is stuff carefully memorized. Mr. Austen Chamberlain has recently published a delightful article on how the great men make their speeches ; and most illuminating, not to say heartening, reading it makes. Will it not bring a new hope into many a study to be told that Joseph Chamberlain often took five days to the composition of a speech, those speeches that appeared to cost him not an effort, and that sometimes by the end of the third day he was no foot further on than when he started : and that in most of our statesmen's homes, apparently, when an effort is brewing, there reigns a solemn and strained hush, with scared private secretaries tiptoeing to and fro, unwilling to attract attention ? But the point now is to note how many of the great orators either memorized, or at least began with that. Disraeli on occasion would recite his whole speech to the Press before delivery ; apparently he carried it nearly word for word in his head. And John Bright, who started on the memorizing system till he swung across to something freer, could repeat his speeches verbatim for some days after their delivery. While the article ends with a delightful story of the guests at a country house fleeing from one alley in the gardens where Hugh Cecil—was it ?—was declaiming a coming speech, into another, only to find themselves face to face with Winston Churchill practising his peroration there.

And the records of the Church tell in the same direction. The tradition of the French pulpit, for example, with its gorgeous if somewhat theatrical oratory, has been to commit, more or less to memory, little though anybody could have suspected it while listening to the outrush of those passionate appeals. And such a delicate judge as Newman quite definitely counsels as the better course for ordinary men, first to write, in order that things may not be vague or unwieldy and disorderly, and then, " mainly, not verbally, to get it by heart." And this upon three grounds. First, that if a discourse is too elaborate and subtle to be delivered without manuscript, it is certainly too subtle and elaborate to be followed without a paper before the hearers too. Second, " for myself I think it no extravagance to say that a very inferior sermon, delivered without book, answers the purpose for which all sermons are delivered more perfectly than one of great merit if it be written and read." And third, that far more preachers than realize it could get across from the reading method to the freely spoken style by the bridge of this partial memorizing.

As to that second point, it may, and I think does, contain exaggeration. To me a read sermon, if well read, is about as effective as the other ; and a good sermon tolerably read much more useful than a bad one well delivered. Coleridge, of course, preferred them read. And some of the most electric preachers have been close readers. Chalmers kept following his manuscript with his finger, line by line, while see-sawing awkwardly with the other hand. So that there is surely not a little to be said for Swift's view, when, in his " Letter to a Young Clergyman," as genial a thing as he ever wrote, he remarks that he prefers a sermon without paper, yet very sensibly concedes that he is satisfied if a man read well and freely, with his head up, not poring over a manuscript so much corrected that he can make little of what he is supposed to have given the week to prepare, with his nose held an inch from the cushion, or popping up and down, for all the world like a schoolboy sneaking

glances at the repetition that he does not
know !

What then should you do, and which
method ought you to adopt ?   No one can tell
you.   Here, too, everyone must be himself,
and choose the style of things that he finds is
best suited to him. Yet may I, without
impertinence, give you my own experience,
for what it is worth.   What the great masters
do is not of vital moment to us average men.
But it does help, I think, when we ordinary
mortals lay our heads together, and tell each
other frankly what we have found from actual
trial. Well, in our fourth year at New
College, Rainy gave each of us an hour's
private interview, in which he talked over our
future, and in so doing brought us, alone
there with him, one by one so far into the
Secret of the Presence that our hearts, awed
as they have rarely been, stood face to face
with God.   For the first half hour, indeed, he
asked questions that revealed a strangely
accurate knowledge of each man.   But in the
second he answered what we had said, waded
in far deeper, and closed with a prayer of

dedication quite extraordinarily moving. One of his questions to me was, " Are you going to read, or preach ? " And I said, " Read." " Why ? " he asked. " Because," I answered, " I am a man of slow mind, and with some love of the beauty of words. And having found those that I like, I should prefer to use them, rather than such rough approximations as might tumble into the memory." " Yes," he said, " write with the utmost care. But I believe that in a few minutes you could reproduce it fairly accurately with no scrap of paper." " But," I questioned, " would not one have the strained, anxious look of a man reading off the back of his head." " Do I look like that ? " he answered, " For that was how I learned to speak. I found that taking up a manuscript which I had written, I could, if I walked up and down (he laid great stress on that) gather it, practically as it stood, though without slavish exactness, into my mind. And I believe that some, you for one, could do that too, quite easily and swiftly and without strain."

" But, sir," I asked, " did you never stick ?"

" Oh, yes, I stuck fast once in the High Church : the whole thing vanished." " And what happened, sir ? " " I very well remember. I looked round, saying to myself, ' There you are, some hundreds of my best friends, all anxious to help me, and not one of you can do a hand's turn for me !' In the end one just went on." Dods, when I told him this, said he was present when it happened, and that the pause was only momentary, and quite imperceptible to the congregation? " I fear," said I, " I could not be so cool as that," and thought no more about it for a dozen years, wrote and rewrote far into the night with an over-anxious carefulness, that was wearing enough then, but for which I am thankful now. And then, urged by some freak, I discovered that for me at least the thing is true, that, if one has written carefully, it can be got up fairly accurately with quite curious ease and exactness, that to walk up and down and read it over, passage by passage each three times, is usually sufficient.

And then there came the war, with no privacy out yonder, and often with no chance to write even the meagrest notes. Once, I remember, back at rest in a place of awful mud and rain, making a sermon sitting on the floor of a hut, with a gramophone going in the centre, with a party playing cards in one corner, another singing psalms in the second, a third entertaining their friends across the floor, and a couple of boys snoring loudly and peacefully beside me! And thus it is that for years now I have never written a sermon, or more than the barest headings, till the Monday after it has been delivered, if even then, for many of them of course drift away. For you have no idea how nearly impossible it is to turn back to the cold porridge, and to get it over! There, then, is a fact to put among the other facts in your brain, to help you to decide what you should do.

That method of which I have been speaking —earnest preparation without writing—does not save much time. If you adopt it for that end, you will finish, and that very quickly, by talking aimlessly and diffusely, without much body or soul either, in a mere sprawling splash of a thing. It means desperate hard work, and absorbed concentration. Bonar Law, who used it, said that it was more tiring to sit in a chair thinking out a speech in this way for an hour, than to walk twenty miles, and often it took him much longer than an hour to get even really begun. Yet I believe that, ultimately, that is the true method for those who can adopt it, and that far more could train themselves to use it than is at all realized.

But at the start what should one do ? If you are a born orator, and I warn you there are not more than, say, two or three in a thousand, and if you are prepared to work hard enough week by week, you might manage without paper from the very first. If you have a lawyer's kind of mind that can get up things quickly and carry them accurately for a time at least, you might find that memorizing method, more or less, a helpful bridge towards something better. But if, on trial, you find it makes you mechanical or straitened —stop it at once. For evidently it is not for you. But most of us, I fancy, with our Scottish minds and Scottish audiences, will be well advised to begin by writing, most of our work at least, with scrupulous care. Denney in his younger days made up his mind that he must do so or " become a haveral " ;—in his case, perhaps, an excess of panic. For the imagination simply will not picture him in that alien part. But for some of us it is a real danger. Better, at first at least, write; and read, as freely as possible, most things.

Even when, later, you take to speaking without paper after most careful preparation, it is always well to have two or three headings with you, with a ring round them to catch the eye. For even the most skilled speakers are subject to incredible lapses of memory. Parker once prepared, as he never prepared, for a speech he was to make at an enormous gathering in Edinburgh to celebrate the Union of the old Free, and United Presbyterian, Churches. It was to be the effort of his life. Yet, when he rose, the whole thing had vanished from his mind! Nor did he ever recover any of it till he had sat down, had to fall back on an old sermon in no way appropriate, and, in short, entirely failed, the one miss of a whole evening of remarkable speaking ! Three headings on a calling card would have saved him from that !

Begin, so I advise, by writing with the utmost care : and keep all you write. For old sermons are invaluable. Even if you never use them, the feeling they are there will prevent fidgetiness in an emergency. I know a man who, when he left his country charge for one in the city, was advised by a distinguished church leader to burn all his manuscripts; and, touchingly obedient, he did it, with the result that he has violently hated that church leader ever since ! For in his rushed tumult of a life, he had always to live on the precipice's edge, with nothing between him and a terribly busy week or, say, some days of illness. For myself, I hate preaching old sermons in my own church, even though they have never heard them there. So much so that, though there must be hundreds of them lying from old days, I have not, I think, preached half a dozen in three years. A sufficiently stupid fact ! For most ministers will tell you that they are thanked as much for old sermons as for new. And naturally so. For there are always people in the church who are nearer the stage at which you stood when you wrote them than they are to you to-day. And it is not true that our present work is always better, though as a rule it ought to be. Wesley hotly denied that it was so with him, declared that many of his old sermons were as good as he could do, and preached some of them, such as " The One Thing Needful," I suppose hundreds of times. On the other hand, Denney maintained that he would not singe a hand to save his whole stock ! But his was a heroic heart. Still, for my part I am never happy or at ease in conscience when at home unless both my sermons are new.

Write too, in part at least, in order to treat the glorious medium in which we work with reverence. We hear much of the appeal of symbolism. But there are no symbols anything like so wonderful as words, these odd things we keep throwing at each other. And beautiful words and finished English win the heart. Style is not idle. It is power. Time

spent upon it is not wasted, the mere suggestion is a crime. For a phrase, an image, an apt
adjective, may bring home to some needy soul
a whole new side of truth, may make it feel
God very near, may win it for the Master.   It
is often through such things that these great
matters happen. It is the added master
touch that makes it vivid, runs it into the
mind, the heart, the conscience.

That pleasant person, Quiller-Couch, asks
us to imagine the parables if they had been
written by Jeremy Bentham. I will do
nothing of the kind! I hold that no really
nice mind could have been visited by such a
horrible suggestion, which, indeed, he tries to
father on FitzGerald. It is, of course, largely
the beauty of our Saviour's way of putting
things that moves us. The story of the
Prodigal might have been written with no
thrill in it at all, the same facts set down dully.
And we can never be too grateful for the
spiritual power that there lies in the literary
glory of the Authorised translation. Souls
innumerable have been saved through that.
And not a little of the pulpit's ineffectiveness

is due to nothing more or less than the
stodginess of its English.

Personally, I am of opinion that rules for
style have a very limited measure of usefulness
—that the most hopeful thing is to read and
re-read the great authors (as Dale kept Burke
always within reach, at his bedhead and the
like), and let their majesty and glory form a
standard for us, which will at least keep us
from being quite as bad as we would certainly
have been without it ; give us a sense of what
is fitting ; of how it should be done, if only we
could do it ; and even help us up a little
nearer to it. That I would urge upon you
with insistence, that, and the excellent
practices which Johnson once told Reynolds
were the means whereby he had attained
to his extraordinary accuracy and flow of
language. " He had early laid it down as a
fixed rule to do his best on every occasion,
and in every company : to impart whatever
he knew in the most forcible language he
could put it in ; and that, by constant
practice, and never suffering any careless
expressions to escape him, or attempting to

deliver his thoughts without arranging them in the clearest manner, it became habitual to him." Believe me, the whole technique of preaching, the whole art of learning how to do it, cannot be put better than that. But, if we are to have rules for style, here are four laws from Schopenhauer, none of them new, though he makes no acknowledgments, yet all of them worth pondering. "The first rule, nay this in itself is almost sufficient for a good style, is this, that the author should have something to say." That was Sir Walter Scott's opinion, almost in the same words, "Get ideas, and words will come." Second, "A man who writes carelessly at once confesses that he puts no great value on his thoughts." That is, of course, what Bishop Butler taught us long ago. Third, "A man who is capable of thinking can express himself at all times in clear, comprehensible and unambiguous words. Those writers who construct difficult, obscure, involved phrases most certainly do not know what it is they wish to say. They have only a dull consciousness of it, which is still struggling to put itself

N

into thought." That was Socrates' teaching.
And fourth, " Truth that is naked is the most
beautiful, and the simpler the expression the
deeper the impression." Turgid language is
not eloquence. For, surely, Morley was right
when he held that the noblest form of that is
one " which dispenses with declamation, a
deep, rapid, steady outflowing volume of
argument, exposition and exhortation."

One thing I would impress upon you
urgently, always to remember that, with the
vast majority of people, it is through their
imagination far more than their reason that
you reach the heart and will ; that if you want
them really to understand, then you must
make them see, almost as if with the bodily
eye. Coleridge had colossal gifts of many
kinds, yet he it was who says, " The primary
imagination I hold to be the living power and
prime agent of all human perception, and as
a repetition in the finite mind of the eternal act
of creation in the infinite I Am." Most of us
can think only in pictures ; and no one needs
to be ashamed of that, though it is true he
shares the trait with children. For all the

very greatest of mankind, those who have most profoundly stirred and changed the world, have possessed minds that worked precisely in that fashion, flashing picture upon picture upon others' vision. Look for proof at the mightiest preachers, Socrates, Buddha, Muhammad, Paul, even at the supreme example, at the teaching of Our Lord and Master, Jesus Christ. The Gospels are a glorious picture gallery: everywhere there is appeal made to the eye; the deepest truths are stated metaphorically; the most profound of human thoughts are made to stand out of the page in living figures. We do not have to think them, for we see them. And we must try to gain some dim far-off approximation to the Master's unique faculty. Because, as Ruskin says, " the greatest thing a human soul ever does in the world is to see something, and to tell what it saw in a plain way. Hundreds of people can talk for one who can think, but thousands can think for one who can see. To see clearly is poetry, philosophy, and religion—all in one." And all real thinkers, in his judgment, become

seers. That I believe is true. The mass of
folk, whether they see or not, possess at least
the faculty of seeing, have imagination, and
it is through that that you are likeliest to
touch them. A preacher's first task is
himself to see what he is to say and describe. If he cannot do that, if he cannot make
a picture of it before his own mind, the likeli-
hood is that he himself does not as yet really
understand, or only muddily at best, and is
not seeing accurately and clear-cut, but
through a fog. And his second duty is to
make the congregation see what he sees. For
a great part of our difficulty is that, through
constant repetition, the gospel story has grown
blurred and dimmed to most people's minds,
and we have got to restore the weathered
colours, to make them vivid and clear, there
before their eyes again, or they will never
feel the wonder and compulsion of it all.

About the Cross, indeed, I never am quite
sure. I have a shrinking feeling that it is best
to leave that heavy veil of the gross darkness
that God's own hands drew over it, unlifted.
Yet if one can do it without loss of

seemliness and reverence, and can paint like Fra Angelico upon his knees, there is no doubt that one can in a few words bring home to people a new sense of the tremendousness of what they have seen so often that they hardly notice it at all. They do not even so much as turn their heads now when passing beside the Cross, which has grown an accustomed object, a thing lost in the familiar landscape, over which their eyes run without being arrested by what has always been there, like the war memorials in the village streets, which people do not notice any longer, though at first they were moved to tears each time they passed. But certainly in other places if you can make the Master, and the scenes about Him, and the promises He uttered, and the mighty works He wrought, vivid and visible, can help the people really to see it all, then one's work is well upon the road to success. But one has not only to imagine oneself into the text, but in addition into the people's lives and places and conditions. Take as an illustration, children's sermons. " I met the children," notes John Wesley, " the most difficult part of our office."

And many will agree with him in that.
" Nothing indeed," as Cecil, whom some have
called the English Pascal, says, " is easier
than to talk to children, but to talk to them
as they ought to be talked to is the very last
effort of ability." And that, as he proceeds
to say, because the first essential is " a
vigorous imagination," a faculty of " throwing
the mind into the habit of children's minds,"
which he maintains, " requires great genius."
Certainly we are getting somewhat better at
it. The so-called children's sermons of, say,
forty years ago are on the whole entirely
unbelievable to us to-day. I would not care
to tell you things that I myself have heard,
having no wish to be branded in your minds as
a consummate liar, and an inartistic one at
that! But we have still far to travel. When
a missionary lands on a new island, he is
surrounded by the populace. There they
are, crowding shyly or truculently round him,
actually touching him ; and yet, near though
they are, they are living in another world from
him, and how to bridge the gulf between them
is his problem. So when you face a class of

youngsters, their knees may be all but touching yours. Yet in that narrow space there yawns all the long waste of years that lie between you and your own distant childhood. And unless you have imagination enough to recall it, or to picture it as it must have been, accurately and in detail, (always that last is most important to the child's mind —have you noticed the extraordinary skill with which Kipling uses it ?—) unless you can think yourself back into that dimly remembered world of childish joys and sorrows and cares and troubles, can see it all again, and move about in it, as you did long ago, you may take the neatest subject, and the cleverest illustrations, as you think, yet never come within sight of the children's minds, you who are living in another world from them, calling from a far distance in an alien tongue. You remember Goldsmith musing on the fable he felt he could write on little fishes. " The skill," he said, " consists in making them talk like little fishes." And when Johnson laughed, he flashed out the retort, " if you were to make little fishes talk, they would talk like

whales." Most so-called children's sermons
do, from sheer lack of imagination.

And so it is with other sermons too. For
real success, to reach the people, we must have
the faculty of thinking ourselves vividly into
their place, their difficulties, their duties,
their temptations, down at the office, or in
the kitchen, or wherever it may be. And if
we lack that gift, we are almost bound to fail;
our voice will reach them, thin and distant;
and they will listen in a puzzled way, trying
to translate it all into the facts of their own
life, with which it seems to have little to do.
It will sound cold and academic and abstract.
Of all possessions, few are more serviceable to
the preacher than a wise and schooled
imagination.

Further, if you wish to be popular these
days, you will be short. There is no manner
of doubt about that. Yet here am I, an
amazing dodo, still surviving from an earlier
age. Behold one, who, when in the pew,
dislikes a short sermon, resenting it as something of an insult, unless indeed it is very bad,
which few Scottish sermons really are. We

all learned, indeed, at the front how much can
be said in fifteen minutes or so, if you waste
no time. And yet is twenty-five or thereby,
say twenty-seven, really too long, especially
in these days when so many folk do not come
back a second time to church? Too long to
bring their rushed minds, almost of necessity
filled with the dust and din of other things,
into the presence of God, and to let some
sense of that sink so far into their memories
that it will follow them, and haunt them, and
tell on them unconsciously all through the
dangers and temptations of the week : too
long to provide something for hundreds of
souls, each one of them with its own individual
needs : too long to rally the discouraged, and
to warn the careless, and to bring new vision
to those whose faith has gone out : too long
to meet the differing urgent claims of all these
different hearts! Too long? To ask the
question is to answer it, if we possess any
imagination, and the slightest faith in the
value of what we are doing. If people
gathered to a political meeting, and the chief
speaker spoke to them only for some quarter

of an hour, they would be annoyed, would
feel with some resentment that he had not
taken them seriously, had dealt much too
cavalierly with the question of the hour, an
Ulster boundary, or such like. But the things
of the soul are far more momentous, and to
be asked to deal with huge unfathomable
facts like the Cross in a few minutes, means
that people are not really interested in these
things. This is of course a snippetty age, with
a snippetty press, and snippetty novels. But
must we preachers follow and be snippetty
too ? " But," answered Klopstock, " that
is the kind of thing every one wants." " True,"
replied Coleridge, " but is it not the business of
a real poet to lift people to his level, not to sink
to theirs ? " It is very questionable whether
Gladstone's law for the making of an orator
holds for the pulpit. " He cannot follow
nor frame ideals : his choice is, to be what
his age will have him, what it requires in order
to be moved by him, or else not to be at all."
That is undoubtedly the road to popularity ;
but, beyond very narrow limits, is it what
our Lord claims from His representatives ?

No doubt at all we can be far too long, are apt to try to pack in far too much, partly from diffidence and a lack of self-confidence, partly from respect for our audience, not least because of being wishful really to effect something for Christ. Yet a real danger to us Scottish preachers is a much too literal interpretation of that saying of Buffon, " every subject is one, and, however vast, is capable of being contained in a single discourse." The desire to be exhaustive can be greatly overdone. Here are three rules for you, culled from three masters. No single quality, in Pope's opinion, is so valuable for good writing as the power of rejecting one's own thoughts. It may be admirable ; but, if it is off the line, let it alone. Again, one of the chief marks of a real preacher, according to Luther, is that he knows how to make an end, does not keep dribbling on and on when he is really finished. And, lastly, Mr. Asquith, himself the finest model of succinct English with never a word used unnecessarily who ever stood up in the House of Commons, says bluntly, " A vast deal of the slipshod and prolix stuff which we are compelled to read or listen to is, of course, born of sheer idleness. When, as so often happens, a man takes an hour to say what might have been as well or better said in twenty minutes, or spreads over twenty pages what could easily have been exhausted in ten, the offence in a large majority of cases is due not so much to vanity or indifference to the feelings of others, as to inability or unwillingness to take pains."

One thing is clear, the hurry of the age has killed oratory everywhere. We are not given time to develop thought and images, as they were long ago, but are asked to snap out the thing, and be done with it. So it is in the House of Commons, and so it is in the pulpit. Effects, such as those produced by Guthrie, when he painted a shipwreck with such minute vividness, that a sailor in the front seat of the gallery leapt up, preparing to jump over for a rescue, and had to be restrained ; or when Whitefield described a blind man, deserted by his dog, stumbling feebly over a desolate moor, and at last groping and hovering unknowingly upon the sheer edge of a hideous precipice, nearer and nearer, till " Good God, he is gone ! " exclaimed Lord Chesterfield, of all men—effects such as these need time in order to develop and produce them—more time than is granted us to-day. That, perhaps, does not greatly matter. It was an eminent authority who remarked, that " Eloquence, without being precisely a defect, is one of the worst dangers that can beset a man." Yet, perhaps, it matters vastly. You remember how Benjamin Franklin went to hear Whitefield, with his mind set against him ; but, as he listened to his fervent appeal for an orphanage, felt he must give the coppers in his pockets, and as the sermon proceeded, saw that the silver too must go, and listening further found that it must be the gold, and in the end had to throw in the whole. Which thing is a parable. Had the sermon been cut short according to the modern standards, the copper was the most there could have been. And we lose things more valuable by far than mere silver and gold by our rushed methods. Men, knowing how short is their time, are apt to preach upon mere prettinesses and to shirk as hopeless the deep things that would awaken the old response and zeal and passion.

Yet, in truth, the length of a sermon has little to do with time. I have stood in the aisle listening to Ian Maclaren for fifty minutes, disagreeing with much he said, but with the pleasure of the last quarter of an hour marred somewhat by the haunting fear that he might stop. While the longest sermon through which I ever hitched and hotched and fidgeted lasted for about nine minutes. It was a glorious old English church, and the curate was a nice boy, but obsessed by a phrase that seemed to fascinate him, " the after-glow of Easter morning." I knew, before I went to church, it was the Sunday after Easter ; and that was all that, with a monotonous reiteration, I was told. It is not really length that worries people : they will listen to the right man long enough. It is lack of interest that bores, and kills attention. And how we are to attempt to avoid that, and other dangers always threatening, is the theme of our last lecture.

DURING these lectures I have been unhappy, unable to look my conscience in the eyes, dogged by the wretched feeling that I have lost even that meagre rag of virtue with which Socrates declared that he concealed his nakedness—that if he did not know, at least he knew he did not know : whereas have not I given folk the right to say " Of course he cannot preach, we all know that ; but the pathetic thing is that apparently he himself has no idea of it, and presumes to talk to others ! " But to-day I am much easier in mind, am dealing with a subject on which really I am entitled to be heard, upon which few indeed can speak with fuller or more accurate knowledge—some bogs and peathags, by one who has been in them all. And if to you, setting out across the moors, there rises a muddied and bedraggled figure, gesticulating violently and bidding you to turn back and go round some other way, if you take his

advice and keep to firmer ground, our gatherings will not have been in vain. " I flatter
myself," says Reynolds, " that from the long
experience I have had, and the unceasing
assiduity with which I have pursued those
studies, in which like you I have been
engaged, I shall be acquitted of vanity in
offering some hints for your consideration.
They are indeed in a great degree founded
upon my own mistakes in the same pursuit.
But the history of errors, properly managed,
often shortens the road to truth.   And though
no method of study that I can offer will of
itself conduct to excellence, yet it may
preserve industry from being misapplied."

Let us then start from this patent and
somewhat disconcerting fact that preaching,
for the moment, appears to effect much less
than one could wish ; that in spite of the huge
mass of earnest preparation, and the vast
weekly expenditure of toil and skill and heart
and strength of innumerable preachers, the
world seems to go stolidly and unconcernedly
upon its heedless way.   The ministry may
not be all that it ought to be, yet its standards

are high. There are, no doubt, lazy, inefficient men among its ranks. A maid of ours from the Western Isles once asked my wife what I did every forenoon in my study, and being told I was preparing for the services, tossed her head. " Oh, is he ? " said she with open contempt. " Our minister at home never needs to study! He knows it all already." She was, one hopes, libelling a worthy man. For our ministers do try.

But, that being so, why is it that far more does not come of it ? What makes our services so largely ineffective, judging at least by visible results ? Well, to begin with, we are faced by the plain fact that when people say they like a preacher, they very often mean simply that they can hear him easily, and with comfort and no strain. That is a first demand. And surely it is a legitimate one. We have come to hear, they say, and if we don't hear, for us everything has failed. We wished to be helped, and instead of that are merely irritated and exasperated. And the better the sermon is, the more annoying is it to folk, barely catching it, to lose it. "Resolved,"

o

wrote Johnson, in his journal for 1765, " if I
can hear the sermon, to attend it, unless
attention be more troublesome than useful."
That latter painful alternative, often enough
in certain churches, falls to unhappy people's
lot.

No doubt the thing can be, and often is,
grossly exaggerated. " It is a strange thing,"
an old man once said to me in all innocence,
" that not one single preacher can speak out
now as all preachers used to do when I was
young." One could not bawl the explanation
into the dulled ears. And once, sitting in the
back row of a great hall, I was listening to
Sir Donald Maclean, an admirable speaker,
but (perhaps he was tired, for it was in the
middle of a General Election), with a trick
now and then of lowering his voice for half a
phrase. Whereat a decent man beside me
became quite furious, declaring that he could
not hear one single word he said. I happened
to be feeling sore upon the point just then,
and turned upon the man, maintaining that
it was simply impossible, if he had average
ears, that he could be missing more than the

last three words or so of every paragraph. " Well," he said, " and how can I make sense of all the rest, if I miss that ! " And I suppose that that is true. You and I forget that our college training has given our minds a certain natural quickness in these things ; an aptitude, shall we say, for getting the general drift of a lecture without attending very closely ? If we miss a word or two, we can instinctively fill in what it is likely to have been, and move on with the speaker. But there are others, slow pedantic creatures, who lose a whole sentence or two puzzling over that missed word, and so keep falling further and further into the rear, till they are fairly lost.

Even so, something may be effected even in their case. My father used to tell of an excited man, standing beside him in the Waverley Market, when Gladstone was speaking, to whom even that wonderful voice failed to penetrate, yet he kept crying in a kind of ecstasy, " It's grand, grand, though I canna hear one word of it." But such enthusiastic souls, so easily satisfied, are not common in church pews. I once heard Rainy, indeed, speaking with enthusiasm of a scholarly man's sermons. "But," said another, " will the simple people to whom he preaches follow him at all ?" " Oh, well," said Rainy, " they will have the comfortable feeling that something very fine is going on." But that is somewhat meagre fare. And, similarly, folk are entitled to much more than the assurance on coming out of church that the sermon that they did not hear was really very noble ! Yet many of us fail them badly there. It is all very well to blame architects (and language can hardly be too strong for them) and churches (and Gothic, lovely though it be, is not really suited to our Presbyterian type of service). But when all is said and done, the real and central fact is that many of us do not know how we should use our voices, and are poor bunglers at a main part of our business. One of the greatest preachers in the world once told me long ago that he attributed any success he had had to this, that whereas his fellow-students spent their days in amassing things to say, and seemed quite careless how they were to say them, he, having studied human nature, felt that the central thing was to know how to speak, and that to speak a poor thing well was much more likely to create impression on men's minds than to speak a fine thing inaudibly. "I am quite sure," he said, "that there is hardly a man in my year whose sermons are not better than mine, but they have never an idea how to use them ; throw away in the pulpit nearly all their labour at their desks." That, I think, is making too clear-cut a distinction. One might both gather things to say, and at the same time learn to say them.

But, in truth, it is nothing short of tragic how much fine work is largely lost and wasted in the pulpit through lack of a little art.

Not that we are to aim at being rhetoricians. A man's delivery must be the one natural to himself. And even that may vary with different types of themes and in different churches. Full of vivid movement in this, one will have none in that, feeling instinctively that only so can one be audible there. Johnson, of course, disliked any action, holding it useful when addressing dogs, but of less and less influence the more reasonable people grow; and in the heat of discussion actually committed himself to sweeping Demosthenes brusquely aside, roundly declaring that " he spoke to an assembly of brutes, a barbarous people," a dark saying that stumbled even Boswell, who remarks shrewdly enough that " reasonable beings are not solely reasonable."

Studied gestures are almost certain to fail with most men in the pulpit. You remember Thackeray's pitiful picture of Charles Honeyman before the looking-glass ! But if your hands leap out of themselves, let them go. Really there is no question of letting. For, if you are really preaching, you won't know what they are doing, will be carried away by your theme, with your whole being emphasizing it. Only you must take heed to the real danger of uncouthness, of being merely violent, and not impressive. The quiet preacher makes the fewest mistakes ; though, on the other hand, the highest peaks are not for him. But all great speakers are restrained. In delivery, as in other things, every one must be himself. Whyte and Dods were bosom friends, yet in their pulpit methods they stood wide as the poles asunder. The one, unconsciously, was a consummate actor, losing himself in his part, and living it, not merely speaking it. To hear him quote that favourite of his, " Lo, this man's brow, like to a title-page," and so on, was to see the thing before one. While Dods stood rigid, with no slightest movement, speaking earnestly but quietly, as if by the fireside among his friends. Each man must be himself.

But to know how to use one's voice is a first essential to real success. Many of us speak too fast. Though, for my part, I stick to it that I prefer quick speaking, and, provided it is audible (Jones of Bournemouth speaks fast but very clearly), maintain that the ideal is, as it were, to burst in with an urgent message, obviously feeling one has news that matters hugely, and not to drop it out, coolly and unexcitedly, as if the people can take it or leave it, it is all the same to me. When one is interested or impressed, one speaks naturally quickly. That day the armistice was in the papers, nobody ran to his wife and said in slow

monotonous staccato, "The—war—is—o—
ver—." Yet that is how one would need to
measure it out in certain churches, to be
clearly heard. If a man speaks too slowly it
gives me subconsciously the impression that
he himself does not greatly care about what
he is saying, does not feel it much, which is to
me much worse than losing a stray phrase or
two. In any case it never seems to occur to
disgruntled people complaining "you speak
too fast," that the obvious answer is "No;
but you think too slowly."

Still, most of us do speak too fast, or at
least too indistinctly, for the mass of people.
When we want to be impressive we are apt
to grow only inaudible. We cannot, for
example, whisper, as an actor can. We drop
our voices too low at the close of sentences :
we bite off the ends of words, and do not spit
out our final consonants. When we wish to
make a point, we raise our voice and shout.
" There is another man," writes Wesley, " who
has killed himself by screaming." We shout,
where real orators speak lower, and more
slowly, and increasingly distinctly. Watch

the politicians, those among them who are masters, how easily and out of nothing they produce immense results, because they know exactly how to use their voices, and, without thinking of it, get effects we miss.

Wesley once took a service along with Whitefield, and remarks with curious complacency, "How wise is God in giving different talents to different preachers! Even the little improprieties both of his language and manner were a means of profiting to many, who would not have been touched by a more correct discourse, or a more calm and regular manner of speaking." Perhaps. Still, I would not trust to that. It seems a little unfair to make God responsible for our gaucheries, and a little unwise to look to them for spiritual success. Far better take pains to lay them aside.

But to wade deeper. Almost the most fatal flaw that can occur in any service is to create an impression of unreality ; that the whole thing is official, and away from life, what is said in churches, but of course not to be taken seriously just as it stands. You

remember how in " Alice for Short " de
Morgan makes the widow say in explanation
of her poring over the story of the Resur-
rection, " You see, my darling, it may be
really true, and not only like going to church."
That is a very terrible saying for us ministers,
who have apparently created in some minds
an impression of unreality in various ways,
not least by a lack of conscience about words,
by talking in a kind of pulpitese, by saying
more than we really mean, heaping it up to
force it home upon the people's mind ; yet,
little though we think it, only making them
incredulous of what we say, and doubtful of
our pulpit veracity.   I well remember going
through the very first sermon that I ever
wrote—it was on " To me to live is Christ "—
and carefully weighing every superlative, to
make sure that it would not be more honest
to stroke that out, and substitute a simple
positive.   That was a wholesome instinct.
If when each new sermon of yours lies before
you finished, you too would run through it,
especially the eloquent passages where you
let yourself go, to make entirely certain

whether it rings strictly true, or whether you have not been overstressing things a bit, would be scrupulous to be strictly honest, you would not only save your own soul from real dangers, but be much more likely to gain the verdict from your hearers' minds. For, in preaching as in golf, pressing does not pay.

I think that we might learn a lesson there from legal speaking. As a rule it is rather too coldly severe for pulpit imitation with exactness. But at its best how admirable is its lucidity and its paucity of words, none wasted, and above all its sincerity, well-knowing as the speaker does, that he dare take no liberties with the bench, that to overstress his case were to invite disaster.

One of the most useful ministers in our church told me that in his college days he had flung away from the whole thing, but that one Sunday, happening to see Dods advertised on a church notice board that he was passing, he turned in, simply for an intellectual treat, but went his way a Christian man. " I did not remember much of what he had said," so he told me; " it was his obvious sincerity in

language and in manner that arrested me.
Here, I felt, was a man who certainly believes
every word he says : who assures me that he
himself has tested Christianity, and has found
that it works. And my mind told me that,
if ever I had seen an honest man, this was he.
If he says it, then I credit it : if he assures me
he has found it entirely dependable, then I
believe him, and I too am going to try it ;
and I did."

It is that sense of reality, the feeling that
this is a witness giving no carried-story but
first-hand evidence, that he himself is too
honest to be doubted, that wins men's verdict
for the faith. In the bygoing, one may add
in a footnote, not without practical interest,
that in that instance part of the effect was
produced by the entire lack of oratory strictly
so called, by the very simplicity with which,
without a single gesture or any art in the use
of the voice, the case was laid before the
congregation, giving the impression of a
confident belief that so strong and convincing
is it, that it only needs to be heard to win its
way. Yet oratory also can produce that

same result. Arthur Balfour, as he then was, set down his impressions of one of Gladstone's speeches, perhaps his very biggest, when he went home that night, and noted as one of its chief powers, " his own obvious conviction that he was right." That effect of sincerity is all-important

On the other hand, take that trying experience that Ruskin tells us he once had in Edinburgh, when a noted preacher there shocked him, when speaking upon fasting, by entirely denying " that there was any authority for fasting in the New Testament " : declared that there were many feasts appointed, but no fasts ; insisted with great energy on the words " forbidding to marry, and commanding to abstain from meats," as descriptive of Romanism, and never once, throughout a long sermon, ventured so much as a single syllable that might recall to his audience's recollection the existence of such texts as Matt. iv. 2 ; vi. 16 ; or Mark ix. 29. This hearer's whole mind was staggered by what he calls " a monstrous case of special pleading " —impossible, he felt, among Romanists, who

are trained to argument, " and are always to
some extent plausible." To be one-sided, to
heap up words that smother the facts, to overpress your case, is a very common mistake of
the pulpit, and a disastrous one. It does not
strengthen things, it weakens them. It
alienates the hearers' minds, it makes them,
and with reason, suspicious of our other
conclusions, it gives them the feeling that,
when heard from the pulpit, words are not to
be held as having their usual value, but are
subject to a huge discount ; till their minds
unconsciously work as ours used to do when
reading a bookseller's catalogue, when we
knew without thinking that 7s. 6d. did not
mean really 7s. 6d., but merely 5s. 8d. cash
down.   So, through over-emphasis here and
there, the pulpit teaches folk to hear without
much discomposure, to minimize and push
aside as an exaggeration all that it says, even
when that is strictly accurate.

I was once minister of St. Matthew's,
Glasgow, and found there an intense affection
for Dr. Stalker, the preacher with whose name
that church will always be associated. Many

things in him I discovered won his people's hearts, but perhaps most of all his honesty; the fact, as they would sometimes say, that he never in prayer or sermon said more than he actually meant and felt. I remember one man telling me how he followed him down to the church on a most wretched day, with inches of slush melting upon the streets, and a persistent drizzle falling through a touch of fog, and how he asked himself, " What will the Doctor do when he reaches the prayer of thanksgiving ? He does not look thankful, creeping along there ahead of me. Will he leave it out : or will he do the formal thing, and for once utter what he does not mean ? " But, as he proudly confessed, he need not have feared. For, when the time came, the prayer opened " O Lord, we thank Thee, that it is not always as bad as this ! " And, starting from that damp wretchedness they were all feeling, he pictured life as it might have been, " always like this," and then kept heaping up the endless joys and gladnesses that God's infinite goodness has thought out for us, and that make this little life of ours so big, so splendid, so inexhaustible, till the soaked folk were lifted clean out of their gloom and dumpishness into a rapture of thanksgiving, and their hearts were up above the clouds in the full sunshine round God's feet. But nothing, so my friend assured me, could have done it, but that first bluntly, almost comically, honest sentence, which faced facts.

Always any touch of posing, unreality, sham, closes the people's hearts, unless they, too, unconsciously are hypocrites. Here above everywhere is it true, as Carlyle used to urge so vehemently, that the first essential is sincerity.

Like other people, you will make mistakes. That is a pity ; nowhere more, nowhere so much, as in the pulpit. Yet, the first and all important matter is, not even that you should always be right, though I beseech you to be careful what you lay down in the name of Christ, but that you yourself obviously mean what you are saying. For there is a real truth in that paradox Mazzini stated about Carlyle," He may deceive himself—he cannot deceive us : for what he says, even when it is not the truth, is yet *true—his* individuality, *his* errors, *his* incomplete view of things— realities, and not nonentities—the truth limited, I might say, for error springing from sincerity in a high intellect is no other than such." When I was at school we had a master who many times a day rapped out almost unconsciously what had become with him a kind of parrot cry, "Above all things be honest." And for the pulpit, as for life, that is the first law.

Further, there is no doubt that we must face the ugly fact that a large part of the reason why people do not come to church is that they find the sermon dull and uninteresting. Stevenson, you remember, in a letter to Crockett, admitted that he was "no great kirkgoer, for many reasons—and the sermon is one of them, and the first prayer another, but the chief and effectual reason is the stuffiness." Perhaps. But you notice that what rushed first into his mind was—the sermon. And first thoughts are apt to be our most honest ones. All this talk about doubts and the like can be much overstated, the real fact is they find us

P

boring. It is not interesting. That is why they stay away. And those who are able to interest them get the people to this day. Just why some prove to be interesting and why some others do not, is a perennial and often baffling problem; but we might all, perhaps, without any baseness or truckling to unworthy tastes, do greatly better in this matter. At all events, no one whose business it is to appeal to his fellow-men and women has a chance of success unless he can interest them. A teacher who lacks that gift may have a dozen admirable qualities, but with them all she will lose the attention of her class and fail: a street politician may be talking much sound sense, and rattling out incontrovertible facts and figures, but if he is not interesting he will have the chagrin of seeing his group melt away: a financier must interest his fellows in his project, or it will never be floated off. And in the pulpit we are not immune from that universal law. I am not talking about tricks more or less cheap, of playing to the gallery, and flashy titles, and the like, all which is of course inexpressibly jarring to a sensitive mind. Even about the whole business of advertising the titles of sermons at all, good men differ. For myself I have no use for it, partly because to me it seems to pander to a mistake only too common without it, that we come to church to listen to a sermon ; whereas, surely, in the main it is to worship God : and partly because never once have I seen a title that induced me to go to hear about it, whereas not seldom I have been scared away elsewhere. In my young days I, too, advertised for a little, very simple titles. It made no difference in the attendance. But there is this fact, not without pathos and practical value, that once, when I was giving what I suppose might be called a course on spiritual therapeutics (horrible jargon of a phrase), how certain sins and habits were actually conquered by certain saints of God, I received letters from folk, mostly women unknown to me, unable to come, telling me that what I had been treating last was their sin, that they were fairly baffled, and begging help.

But to get back to the main stream, we must

try to be interesting. Whatever else we may possess, without that we fail, precisely as Spenser, for all his genius, cannot carry us through the glory of the " Faerie Queene," because, as Macaulay has it, with all its splendour of massed successes, it has one fault—tediousness, and that one makes the cloyed mind turn back. It is a very little and a very weary company that plods on to the very end. And that is often where the pulpit stumbles. Bunyan gives us a passing glimpse of an unfortunate being, " a young woman, whose name was Dull." Ah ! poor soul, can't you see her, flat-faced, flat-footed, a mere vacant lump of a thing ? Too many preachers spring from her family, and are her full brothers—they, too, are dull.

And, being dull, why should folk listen to us ? Don't you remember how Johnson, meeting Fox in the club, the latter started speaking about Catiline's conspiracy, of all prosaic subjects. " So," says Johnson calmly, " I withdrew my attention, and thought about Tom Thumb." And quite right too. When in the pew I, too, have had occasion to with-

draw my attention : and one wonders sometimes when preaching whether, attentive and
absorbed though all the faces seem, the minds
are really following, or have reverted to some
other subject, some Tom Thumb ! They give
us our chance. If we cannot hold them, it is
our own fault. We must be interesting.

Not that to that end we are to adopt
any desperate expedients. These are to
be avoided—humour, for instance, by nine
hundred and ninety-nine men of us out of an
average thousand. I have heard Wesleyans,
who often have a very happy type of service,
introduce it very naturally. And there is no
possible reason in logic why children, gathered
into their Father's house to hear about the
most glorious thing in the world, should be
grave and sober-faced. For one preacher
here and there it may be possible, though even
for him it is apt to prove a temptation. A
great church leader who loved John McNeil
hinted to him that perhaps he was tending to
overdo this side of things. And that big
soul replied, " You know the things I say, but
you don't know the things that come to the

tip of my tongue that I keep back." For
most of us it will not do, if not for the reason
that Swift gave, " I cannot forbear warning
you in the most earnest manner against
endeavouring to wit in your sermons, because
by the strictest computation it is very near
a million to one that you have none "; then for
this other, that for most of us it is not seemly,
not helpful, not conducive to the deepest
things.

No, surely the way to be interesting is to
talk of interesting things, of life and its glories
and its dangers, of the temptations they are
sure to meet, of the help that Christ can give
them in their struggle, of God's strange love
for them and unquenchable faith in them.
Talk to them of big things like that, real
things that touch them closely, of their life,
their problems, their Christ, making them
feel that He is theirs, and, because we are all
interested in ourselves and everything that
touches us, they will be sure to listen.
Whereas, if we meet them with mere abstrac-
tions, and theorizings, and speaking on the
finer shades of doctrine, it is far away from

their whole world, and they quickly lose step with us, and turn away, feeling wearily, as Mr. Asquith says he does about art criticism in the mass, that "it consists, to a large extent, of the unilluminating discussion of unreal problems in unintelligible language." Which raises the next point, that we must speak in English, and not in a kind of bastard speech, a weird religious jargon, that means very little to the ordinary mind. What annoyed Foster in his day has vanished, but another patois has grown up to take its place. No doubt, as we were all taught long ago, all language is fossil poetry and fossil philosophy. But no words ossify so quickly into meaningless things that make really no impression on the hearer's minds as religious phraseology. I should say that to talk in a sermon about eschatology is in itself a proof of incompetence. Many a devout soul will be upon the right hand at the last who has no idea what you mean. And after all, you can say what you are trying to say much better in plain ordinary words. Always eliminate terms like justification, and take the trouble to translate that which now rushes past the ear like a mere empty wind into the thought that lies behind it.   If a philosopher has to resort to obscure technical words not in the dictionary, his thought is suspect.   And if you cannot speak to folk in their own mental language, then there is something wrong.   Why should people have to sit, painfully translating in the back of their heads from what is to them a foreign tongue they do not fully follow ?   You can say all you have to say in straightforward English.   Shakespeare, at all events, made shift to stutter out a thing or two.

Moreover, you can do much to lighten things and to increase your grip upon your hearers' minds by apt and vivid illustration.   Intellectual people, or at least those who would fain be taken for that, may affect to despise that.   You do not need to care.   The Gospels are crammed full of illustrations ; indeed, as Mr. Gauld once said to me, "when you come to think of it, little of Jesus' teaching has survived except the illustrations."   And when you recall a sermon of, say, ten years ago, is it not the illustrations round which your

memories are apt to gather ? It is quite
wonderful, for example, how a good quotation
helps. Swift indeed differs, avers that " you
cannot be too sparing except from Scripture
and the primitive writers of the church."
Which is, indeed, the Church of England ideal
to this day. Why, I have never been able to
imagine, except on the assumption that the
Holy Ghost has fallen dumb these later
centuries. You will find a vast deal better
worth while quoting than the primitive writers
of the church ! Of course your quotation must
be really apt. A thing dragged in without
appositeness, or a hackneyed commonplace,
is worse than useless, can be an affliction not
easily borne. It is indeed a thousand pities
that certain old stagers that have been cruelly
overworked far, far too long could not, like
the one hoss shay, fall to pieces and sink
bodily into oblivion. But a thing new and to
the point and vivid, cleverly introduced, pins
the attention, and at once revives a fading
interest. There seems, I admit, small use in
setting out to look for relevant and striking
things. But if you have read at all, they

ought more and more to come trooping
uninvited into your memory of themselves.
The real difficulty by and by is to make your
selection of the various applicants. Others
have to be rejected by the shovelful.

And when you quote, as a rule, give the
name.   To leave it anonymous, to speak
vaguely of " the poet," is to invite wandering
of thought.   " Now, who said that ? " the
mind asks, and goes off on a quest of its own.
And surely to invite that is bad tactics.

A little thing taken out of real life will
always make folk listen, especially if you
can say " I once saw," or the like. For
Carlyle is quite right. Somehow there is an
odd fascination about an actual fact, " this
happened, this I heard."

But is it not grotesque that we should need
to look for ways of interesting, we who possess
far the most fascinating theme in the wide
world ? Yet there is no doubt we obscure its
glory, dim its splendour, make it, for some
minds, a fairly dull affair !

When Coleridge visited Klopstock, the old
poet declared with emphasis that he thought

that the blank verse of Milton was greatly inferior to that of Glover—G.L.O.V.E.R.—whoever he may be. Whereupon our man, not a little taken aback, pressed the matter, to discover in the end that the confident old critic had read Milton only in a prose translation ! It is a very prosaic and pedestrian translation we give the world of Jesus Christ. If they could see the original in all its beauty, they would have to feel the thrill and glory of the faith.

For one thing, are we nearly joyous enough in our services ? The New Testament is an amazingly happy book. Yet would anyone fasten on that as the characteristic of our times of worship ? In the Epistles we are moving among people whose hearts are aglow, because they have lit upon a glorious discovery that has transformed all life for them, made it an infinitely richer thing, brought what had always been impossibilities within their reach. But is that really the impression produced on the mind by the average sermon ? Tolstoy told us that he became a Christian because he saw that the

men and women round about him who
believed in the faith received from it a power
that enabled them to face life and death with
peace and joy.   That, indeed, is how the faith
is usually propagated.   But do you and I
know Christ well enough to give the impression, when we speak of Him, of this assurance
and fearlessness and happiness ?

Or again, do we succeed in bringing out the
element of glorious adventure there is in the
faith, the chivalry and gallantry that are
required for it ?   It was to daring spirits that
our Lord appealed in the main, the very
people who are apt to turn from Christianity,
as we present it, as from a very dull and tame
affair that in no way attracts them, and that
seems to have nothing in it that calls to the
bigness of their nature.   For to them the
church calls up, not anything heroic, but the
stale smell of tea meetings.   As Jesus Christ
defined it, religion is a constant audacity of
valour.   Always He kept underlining a certain
recklessness of courage and self-sacrifice as a
first requirement.   " But," said a man to
Wesley in his missionary days, " to live out

this faith you preach, one would need to be as bold as Alexander." But we have so dimmed it that the very faith which has a record of glorious unselfishness and bravery that not patriotism itself can match, is pushed aside as an unexciting, drab, uninteresting thing.

Our appeal to men has been far too timid, our call upon them much too diffident. Our Lord, who knew men, never made things easy for them, feeling that is the way to lose them, not to win them. You put a shilling more upon a tax, and there is uproar every-where and much hot discontented talk. You claim men's sons, men's lives, men's everything in a great war, " and here they are," they cry eagerly, " and now what more can we do for you ? " Man is a greater creature than we think ; and it is because, unlike the Master, we pitch the appeal to them too low that they find us uninteresting, and that we leave them so unmoved.

All which runs up into this, that in preaching our psychology is often desperately faulty. Take an example. To concentrate the hearers' attention on their sins is a mistake, and not likely to produce much spiritual profiting. Sometimes, of course, it must be done; and, I admit, I think, that in our preaching nowadays we do not show a due horror of sin, are much too light-hearted over it. But I believe the way to win men from their sins is, not to keep them dwelling upon these, which any psychologist will tell you is likely to result only in them sinking in deeper into their minds and consciousness and being, to make things harder for them than before, but to speak to them about that Jesus who can save from sin, them from their sins, using these last only as an avenue that leads the mind straight to Him, and leaves them face to face with Him and at His feet. You must of course be perfectly frank and honest, you must not mince matters, nor gloss over ugly facts. And you need never do so in our country. For did not Wesley set it down over and over, " I never knew any in Scotland offended by plain-dealing. In this respect the North Briton (whoever he may be) is a pattern to all mankind." " What excuse have ministers in Scotland (ah ! that's better) for not delivering the whole counsel of God, when the bulk of the people not only endure, but love plain-dealing ? ''

That is accurate. As the South Briton saw, we Scottish people like to hear our preachers facing their folk unafraid, and hurling the blunt, biting truth at them. We actually feel a fearful joy in listening to grim facts which we know to be true. Though that, perhaps, is not so certain now, as it was twenty years ago. Yet sure I am that the really effective way to wean men and women from their sins is to talk to them of the Saviour, to make Him vivid to them, to hold up the amazing promises, to let them see their names written across them, and so to bring a new, wild, glorious hope to people who were down and beaten and discouraged and not really trying any more. Fail there, and you may be a true and impressive moralist, but you lack that touch, that something, that means Christ.

And this is not a little matter, a pedantic point. Rather the whole course of our Scottish religion has been marred by the neglect of it. Our spiritual literature is on the whole not first-rate. And that because it is by far too introspective, and nervous, and self-centred, and fidgety. Get your people— tempted, sinful, disheartened—to look away from their own sores and suppurating wounds into the face of Jesus Christ. That is their only chance, and you are there to bring it near to them.

And, further, there is this that I would say. Do not begin to preach, much at least, too soon. " I always feel some apprehension for the destiny of those who in their youth addict themselves to the composition of verses," wrote Wordsworth. And I confess that I feel the same apprehension about those who do much preaching very young. I am of course talking merely of average men. One does not presume to try to cabin genius within bars and rules. An early start does give a certain knack, no doubt, which may deceive an unwary congregation, a kind of glibness which enables its possessor to shoot ahead in the beginning. But student days ought to be given mainly to hard study, and to absorbing everything that can help in our work. And if, impatient with what seems doctrinaire and abstract and away from the real centre of things, eager to work for Christ, to do something for Him that tells, we take too soon to more than occasional preaching, and neglect our daily tasks, we are all too likely to lie stranded and aground in a few years, or to adopt faults and habits not easily remedied, or, perhaps worst of all, to drift into a way of strained and not quite honest speech, of talking beyond our experience. Francis Thompson laments, in a beautiful poem, that he began to sing too soon, and therefore has strayed into foolishness, means some day to try again, hopes to do better by and by when he is ready. But

> " Meantime the silent lip,
> Meantime the climbing feet."

That is not a quotation that exactly meets your case. For you must take your share of Christian work, and are here among other things expressly to begin to learn to preach. Yet it is near enough to the facts of your position to be worth careful pondering.

Much more ought to be said, but our time is away. It is a great life you are facing, let your sphere be what it may : whether yours be some popular ministry with crowded pews, or a grim wrestle, buried somewhere among the grey tides of men and women surging through the sordid streets of some depressing East End slum, where the real heroisms of the church are hidden away—and sometimes I could almost curse the church for its failure to back these valiant spirits bravely facing the almost impossible odds against them—or a life planned on a much smaller scale in a wee congregation lost among the hills. Never despise that last. For it is out of such that much of the best life-blood of the church is pumped continually into the great congregations in the cities. And the influence of preachers there, facing a handful week by week, spreads far. A man I know once made a rough census of the origin of the more prominent religious people in his city, and was amazed to discover what a huge proportion of them the church owes to the tiny country congregations. And Donald Fraser told us once how, on a journey home from Central Africa, at almost every place he touched, he came on some one from the insignificant village in which he was reared. No minister to-day but has a parish wide as the world itself.

A botanist, discovering a rare flower growing thickly all along the margins of one of our Scottish rivers, followed it back and back up a side stream, and then along a tributary of that in its turn, until at long last the trail ended high among the lonely hills in the garden of a ruined shepherd's cottage beside a tiny burn. There it was, in that far-off, forgotten, hidden spot that the original plant had caught and seeded itself, and the winds and waters running past had done the rest. You, too, will make a difference in Scotland, will sow seeds, however small your sphere may look, which the winds of God and the currents of life will carry far. Great place or little place, how glorious a work it is! Do you remember that old incident that so delighted Carlyle, how in wild days in Scotland Sir David Ramsay met Lord Rea.

" Then," said his lordship, " well, God mend
all ! " " Nay, by God, Donald, we must help
Him to mend it," said the other. That is our
honourable task ; in our generation it is
upon you and me God leans. And, as Carlyle
himself put it in words as thrilling as any
that he ever penned : " Here on earth we
are as soldiers fighting in a foreign land, that
understand not the plan of the campaign,
and have no need to understand it, seeing
well what is set to our hand to be done. Let
us do it like soldiers, with submission, with
courage, with a heroic joy ; whatsoever thy
hand findeth to do, do it with all thy might.
Behind us, behind each one of us, lies six
thousand years of human effort, human
conquest. Before us is the boundless time,
with its as yet uncreated and unconquered
Continents and El Dorados, which we, even
we, have to conquer, to create : and from the
bosom of eternity there shine for us celestial
guiding-stars."

" What then is the sum of the whole
matter ? " asked Mr. Asquith in closing his
Rectorial Address in Glasgow. And he

answered very grandly in his final way, " For the moment you here can concentrate your-selves on the things of the mind, installed as you are in this citadel of knowledge. But after these student days are over, the lives of most of us are doomed to be immersed in matter. If the best gift which your Univer-sity can give us is not to be slowly stifled, we must see to it that we keep the windows of the mind, and of the soul also, open to the light and air. We must take with us into the dust and tumult, the ambitions and cares, the homely joys and sorrows, which will make up the texture of our days and years, an inextinguishable sense of the things which are unseen, the things which give dignity to service, inspiration to work, purpose to suffer-ing, a value immeasurable and eternal to the humblest of human lives." Ah, gentlemen, glorious though that is, your office and your privilege is one far higher still. For it is yours, not only to retain that inextinguishable and ennobling sense of unseen things in your own minds, but to be week by week the living fires at which others, for whom it is flickering wildly in the gusts of life, or in whom it is all but out, black, cold, can and will rekindle and renew it.

" Provided," he proceeds, " we live in this temper and spirit, it matters comparatively little whether we take high or low views of what man's efforts can actually achieve. There is a noble optimism which, in spite of all disappointments and misgivings, holds fast to the faith in what man can do for man. There is also a noble pessimism which turns in relief from the apparent futility of all such labour to a keener study and a fuller understanding of the works of God." And with that he passes to that prayer of Bacon at the opening of the Instauratio Magna, which you and I might make our own : " Thou, after Thou hadst turned to behold the works which Thy hands fashioned, didst see that all of them are very good, and Thou didst rest.   But man, when he turns to the works made by his hands, sees that they are all vanity and vexation of spirit.   Nor for him is there any rest.   Yet, since it is in Thy works that we shall labour, make us to be sharers of Thy vision, and Thy Sabbath calm."

Yes, gentlemen, and we can pray that hopefully. For let us remember always that we serve a wonderful Master, who does exceeding abundantly above all that we can ask or think, who gives, not, indeed, always what we asked of Him, yet very wonderfully, who can make even the most splendid and audacious of your day-dreams look how faded, tashed, and shabby side by side with the realities that He will grant you in their place.

Gentlemen, I thank you for your patient courtesy. I wish you God-speed in your life and work. I pray that at the end of it, when you stand much ashamed at the poor little that you have achieved, that there is only this to show for the life God planned, it may be given you to hear His " Well done, good and faithful servant," and be, not cast aside as useless, but—is it not the one reward we covet ?—set, as one tried and found serviceable, to some even higher task.

AFTERWORD

Still in Christ's Stead

In few countries over so long a time has the ministry of the Word been so highly prized and so conscientiously exercised as in Scotland. What is remarkable about Scottish preaching is the long continuity of a very distinct tradition beginning with John Knox and continuing through all the vicissitudes of a rather tumultuous history down to our own day. Scottish preaching has always had great variety, and yet it has consistently emphasized the exposition of Holy Scripture with a remarkable combination of high seriousness, evangelical passion, and solid learning.[1]

Although Arthur John Gossip (1873–1954) has been "a long-time in the Father's House," he remains a meaningful model for ministry in a war-torn world for those who are servants of the Word.

---

1. Hughes Oliphant Old, *The Reading and Preaching of the Scriptures in the Worship of the Christian Church* (Grand Rapids: Eerdmans, 2004), 5:429.

My fascination with A. J. Gossip began in 1979 when my brother, Mark, then a parish minister, insisted I read a sermon titled "When Life Tumbles In, What Then?" After a reluctant reading of this ancient sermon, I became keenly aware that Gossip was, as William Barclay suggested, "one of the world's supreme preachers."[2] Barclay then said, "Gossip lived closer to God than any man I have ever known." Gossip certainly bore the title *The Scholar as Preacher* in grand Scottish style as he modeled a learned and loving ministry in the foxhole at The Front, behind the sacred desk in the church, and in the lecture hall of the university.

It was the reading of this sermon that launched my lifetime love of the Scottish pulpit. In fact, this pastor, preacher, and professor bequeathed a literary legacy that is second to none in the study of the preachers of Scotland: four volumes in T&T Clark's The Scholar as Preacher series; several fine exegetical works; one penetrating work on prayer; and here, *In Christ's Stead*—the 1925 Warrack Lectures on Preaching delivered to divinity students at Aberdeen, Edinburgh, and Glasgow. It was in the reading of these lectures (along with James S. Stewart's *Heralds of God*) that both propelled me into and have kept me in the ministry. It is my hope that a serious, sincere, and sus-

---

2. William Barclay, *Testament of Faith* (London: Mowbray, 1975), 13.

tained reading of *In Christ's Stead* may produce the same effect in the scholar-preachers in our own time.

Thanks to Dr. Calvin Phillips[†] (Emmanuel School of Religion, Johnson City, Tennessee) for writing the foreword to *In Christ's Stead*. It is to Dr. Phillips, and his family, that this re-issue is dedicated.

Thanks also to The Very Rev'd. W. J. G. McDonald (Edinburgh) and Ian R. MacDonald (Aberdeen) for their many letters and continued support of the study of Scottish preaching.

Thanks additionally to my beloved and patient professors: Ronald J. Allen, Hughes Oliphant Old, Wayne Shaw, and Bruce Shields, who have taught me, through witness and word, the love of God and an ever-increasing love of the art of preaching.

Thanks, again and again and again, to both Rob Clements and Bill Reimer of Regent College Publishing for noting the importance of a reissue of this classic text on Scottish preaching.

Thanks always for Barb, Garrett, and Kiersten Grace— God's triple gift of undeserved love.

Last, a word of enduring gratitude is directed to my own dear minister and father in the faith Dr. Richard D. Hogan, who, for thirty-one years, stood "in Christ's stead" shepherding the people of God with integrity of heart. With skillful hands he humbly and lovingly led (Ps. 78:72) our congregation "to the praise of God's glory" (Eph. 1:12). Thank you, RDH, for both believing in and loving me as I remain your "Timothy"—and remain in Christ's stead.

Kurt Iver Johanson
Pastor, Pleasant Grove Christian Church
Dallas, Texas

ARTHUR JOHN GOSSIP

A Selected Bibliography

From the Edge of the Crowd: Being Musing of a Pagan Mind on Jesus Christ. Edinburgh: T&T Clark, 1924.

In Christ's Stead. London: Hodder & Stoughton, 1925.

The Galilean Accent: Being Some Studies in the Christian Life. Edinburgh: T&T Clark, 1926.

The Hero in Thy Soul: Being an Attempt to Face Life Gallantly. Edinburgh: T&T Clark, 1928. *"When Life Tumbles In, What Then?"—the first sermon Gossip preached at Beechgrove Church, Aberdeen, after the dramatic and sudden death of his wife—is included in this work. This sermon may indeed be one of the most important sermons of the twentieth century.*

"On the Preaching of the Cross." *The Expository Times* (July 1931): 443–46.

Experience Worketh Hope: Being Some Thoughts for a Troubled Day. Edinburgh: T&T Clark, 1945.

"The Whole Counsel of God: The Place of Biblical Doctrine in Preaching." *Interpretation* (July 1947): 325–40.

In the Secret Place of the Most High: Being Some Studies in Prayer. New York: Charles Scribner's Sons, 1947.

Milton Keynes UK
Ingram Content Group UK Ltd.
UKHW011316141223
434366UK00001B/107

9 781573 833899